RUN
in My
SHOES

RUN
in My
SHOES

*The Journey of Understanding Race and Prejudice
in America as Seen by an African American*

Phillip Bell, Jr. MA

Primix Publishing
East Brunswick Office Evolution
1 Tower Center Boulevard, Ste 1510
East Brunswick, NJ 08816
www.primixpublishing.com
Phone: 1-800-538-5788

Published by Primix Publishing: 01/28/2026

ISBN: 979-8-89194-571-5(sc)
ISBN: 979-8-89194-572-2(e)

Library of Congress Control Number: 2025920112

Any people depicted in stock imagery provided by iStock are models, and such images are being used for illustrative purposes only.

Certain stock imagery © iStock.

Because of the dynamic nature of the Internet, any web addresses or links contained in this book may have changed since publication and may no longer be valid. The views expressed in this work are solely those of the author and do not necessarily reflect the views of the publisher, and the publisher hereby disclaims any responsibility for them.

TABLE OF CONTENTS

AUTHOR'S NOTES

To Run In My Shoes—my pace since childhood. To win races, run past defenders, to stay ahead of the team, spiritually, mentally and physically. To Run In My Shoes—this phrase also outlines the pace one must set to overcome adversity, to fully understand the role of prejudice in the past, to look forward, to have the faith and courage to make a positive change for the future.

As an African-American male, born in 1957, I have witnessed a wealth of hatred and prejudice, however, I have also enjoyed love, hope and the sweet promise of a better tomorrow. To fulfill this promise, we must first fully understand and acknowledge the past.

To Run In My Shoes, is three-fold in its attempt to provide a comprehensive account of the origins and chronology of prejudice and racism of African-Americans beginning with the 17th Century. It is also a venue to share personal insights, observations, warnings and true concerns. And finally, it provides positive suggestions, proven methods and pro-active plans to improve overall racial attitudes within the American social and economic infrastructure.

Although my life experiences have been seen through the eyes of an African-American, the curse of prejudice is not unique to just that of the African-American. Everyone has seen the legacy of hate, greed, prejudice and evil.

As we attempt to strive towards survival of mankind in this next millennium, let us know the truth of our past mistakes and shift focus to what brings us together, rather than what separates us.

May God Bless You

INTRODUCTION

Man's quest for justice. This struggle to overcome social injustices, religious intolerance, racial discrimination and segregation did not begin in the 20th Century in the United States. Actually from ancient times to the present, the struggle for rights has been the case of countless social and political conflicts and will continue to be the same.

The Founding Fathers knew that slavery was a mockery of human rights. The two systems could not exist side by side. From time to time many interpreted the Constitution for their own purposes and America became a segregated nation.

The struggle still continues . . .

Surveys of Afro-American History

CHAPTER 1

A SURVEY OF ORIGINS OF RACIAL PROBLEMS AMONG BLACKS AND WHITES IN AMERICA PRIMARILY THE 17th CENTURY TO THE 20th CENTURY

OUTLINE

I. Introduction
II. Origins of the Slave Trade
III. Black Presence before the Civil War
IV. Discrimination and Segregation after the Civil War
V. Racial Problems after the Civil War
VI. Conclusion
VII. Bibliography

I. INTRODUCTION

Through the annuals of time, various sections of the planet were inhabited with many different people; however, in America, two major groups of mankind were fused together. The darker Africans were brought to white settlements during the triangular slave trade, to serve as slaves . . . branded by color and marked as a cursed being. This scenario does not enhance the quality of life in a country whose legacy of history is one of justice and equality. My study attempts to succinctly re-examine the historical origins of racial problems of the several groups in a chronological framework from the Afro-American presence in American history and to uncover some of the subtle remnants of the influence and impact of racial diversity on the socioeconomic and political development during the era of integration and post-integration.

Throughout the work, a central theme should indicate the presence of fear, envy, greed, ambition, and master-servant relationships. This is especially true during slavery and the reconstruction periods (1619-1877). The writer notes that while scholars and researchers agree on many facets, many diverse opinions and seemingly questionable views are expressed. It is now time to contribute a series of programs, proposals, and counseling strategies which might assist the youth of today to address many of their concerns on issues still significant, yet often dormant or subtle in American society.

A careful search of literature under the general heading of Afro-American history with a special focus on race problems has helped the writer to understand many of the causes of problems which linger though technological development has been rapid and widespread. A clear, detailed systematic attempt to trace changes and hasten positive action is important to enlarge global awareness on the part of the uninformed or misguided sectors of various persons of the races.

II. ORIGINS OF THE SLAVE TRADE

From the first church-sanctioned European incursions and invasions in Africa to recent volcanic civil rights eruptions in cities across America, this study traces much of the economic and political aspects of world growth and development which has led to continual bitterness and strife between whites and non-whites. From the very beginning, racism has separated and segregated the two groups on American soil. The scholar, must of necessity, examines the roles played by the influences of such men as Jefferson, Madison, Lincoln and Johnson. Their speeches, writing or thoughts are on the record for interpretation. Historians constantly find themselves in a dilemma, and the new breed is taking the foreground casting shadows and doubts, posing new questions on what has been accepted as gospel. A cursory glance of the writer's annotated, bibliography calls forth not only scholars of the old school but new and qualified leaders of distinction. Scholars have labored long over the role and the responsibility of these elite groups, and the relationship to the socioeconomic status of one of the minority groups in the United States.

Scholars agree that one of the major reasons why a white supremacist idea and non-white servantile doctrine took root so tightly into the American fabric can be seen in attitudes of slave dealer groups. For example, in the year 1442 Pope Eugenia IV granted Henry of Portugal permission to deal in slave trading. In 1452, Pope Nicholas V gave general powers to King Alfonso of Spain to enslave those "pagans" or Africans who did not know of Christ. It was the granting of the Vatican office of these powers, which helped to perpetuate the permanence of the slave trade.

In an attempt to uncover information regarding the creation of supremacists viewpoints in the European culture that influenced the institutions of slavery in America, the writer located the writings of Dr. Martin Bernal. He was interested in the influence of Egyptian civilization on Greek culture. Bernal examined many sources and highlighted several examples of the influence of Egyptian civilization. He mentioned architecture noting that the Temple Secura was constructed over five hundred years before the Parthenon, one of the prototypes of Western culture. Irrigation techniques, philosophy, art, astronomy, religion, science, and medicine were attributed to the accomplishments of the early Egyptians.

Dr. Bernal concludes that with the tracing of these achievements in the 16th century, several European countries, particularly Germany, began to actively distort the historical accounts, which were so significant for the black race. He concluded by stating that many of the misguided theories propounded by historians had its origins during this time in history.

The Vatican soon lost hope of the control over the slave trade because of its increased popularity and profitability. There was indeed little comparison of the treatment between the African and whites, soon to be called 'indentured servants'. Cargo ships were built and manned without regard for health or welfare. Statistics on death of the unfortunate voyages were estimated at close to one hundred million. Many Africans chose suicide, while others died of malnutrition and disease.

Throughout the slavery decades, the church turned its back towards the institution of exploitation. Blacks were subjected to hard labor, wretched conditions, poor food, and inhumane treatment. The black survivors of the middle passage were torn from their families, reduced to chattel or property, and placed in captivity. However, many managed to survive this harsh life, some escaped, and others fled seeking refuge in other sections or regions of America, Canada and Africa.

III. BLACK PRESENCE BEFORE THE CIVIL WAR

Historical facts note that blacks entered the United States particularly during the year 1619 at Jamestown, Virginia. It was however much earlier, that slavery was introduced into the European settlements. These persons were also identified as 'indentured servants'. The Swedish social scientist Gunnar Myrdal critically examined the revolutionary period. He argued that America needed certain ideas, attitudes, and policies to defend or to establish a national creed.

For the blacks during this period, there was a lack of basic freedoms that were afforded to the whites. They, however, attributed their best for the young nation behind the background of Crispus Attuck's sacrifice; the colonies with half a million slaves supported the idea that "all men were created equal and were endowed by their Creator with certain unalienable rights". Although they entered the war it was not for their own land but for the land that enslaved them.

Many important figures in the colonies spoke or wrote out against slavery. James Otis and Thomas Paine were eloquent speakers against the tyranny of slave holding. The wife of John Adams stated: "It always appeared a most iniquitous scheme to me to fight ourselves for what we daily rob and plunder from those who have as good a right to freedom as we have." Gunnar chose the rather brilliant statement: "Is it not nearer the truth to say that no man was ever born free and two men were ever born free and equal? Man is born to subjection. One role of the natural man is to dominate or to be subservient."[6] In fact, many argued that slavery was necessary in order to establish equality and liberty for whites only. The Creed was not enacted to apply to Blacks.

Racists pointed out the foundation of the American Creed developed out of the epoch of enlightenment when America was building its political structure. Due to varying feelings, and a lack of legislative momentum, during the three decades leading to the Civil War, any elaborate ideology was contrary to a democratic creed. It was a precarious situation where in racists attempted to defend their political and civil institutions, gain lands Westward, and control all commercial profits.

IV. DISCRIMINATION AND SEGREGATION AFTER THE CIVIL WAR

The growth of discrimination in America developed into more sinister and diabolical forms throughout the 1800's. In essence, many scientific and literary figures began to produce rather significant works and studies about supremacy. One of the more controversial figures of the 1850's was a Philadelphia scientist Dr. Avery Morton. This scientist had a collection of skulls that he had classified, labeled and organized into an array of evidence concerning the differences in races. His procedure of buckshot to the skull was measured to determine skull size. From his work, he concluded that he had discovered the key to the riddle of the basic differences of mankind. Dr. Avery Morton carried his studies to Europe. There he showed what he called a perfect specimen. "It was the cranium of a woman who had lived in the mountain region of Southeastern Europe. This skull became the inspiration for the "Caucasian race".

Dr. Avery Morton studied and categorized skulls on other cultures, but held the "Caucasian skull" as the ultimate in perfection. "He described the people of yellow complexion as Mongolian race. He classified the brown or red races as the Malay race.

The bottom rank was assigned to the Black race, labeled the Ethiopian race. Or, the lowest grade of humanity".

Over the decades, various scholars and scientists wondered how Dr. Avery Morton had arrived at his "amazing" conclusion. Many persons however, did not question his findings or statements. In certain schools and associations he was held as being the foremost authority on race. Dr. Josiah C. Nott, a founder of the American School of Anthropology, was one of many scientists who agreed with Dr. Avery Morton.

Dr. Nott, a lecturer, spoke to slave-owners frequently, noting the importance of white superiority and black inferiority. He expounded on the notions of total separation of races for living with the plantation system of the south. Hirch states the term "Mulatto" was coined by Dr. Nott. Its origin being taken from the root word Mule, referring to a person of mixed parentage. He insisted on racial purity.

Dr. Nott and Dr. Avery Morton enlisted support from Dr. Louis Agassiz, a noted Harvard professor and international intellectual. Agassiz began to subtly argue that it was wrong to ascribe a common center or origin to all living beings on earth. His viewpoints were diametrically opposite to the biblical idea of a brotherhood of man. He insisted that man originated in more that one place. Thus, because of the influences of major studies by Dr. Avery Morton and Dr. Nott, supported by persons like Agassiz, the question of slavery in America was justified on pseudo-scientific grounds. It was truth that people of color and non-color were from different biological species with separate origins. New studies gave rise to the notion of social Darwinism that had developed as a result of the scientific community's justification of racial separation. Here was a distorted theory taken out of context used to justify the institutions of slavery, poverty, colonialism and race hatred.

V. RACIAL PROBLEMS AFTER THE CIVIL WAR

One of the greatest problems of the researcher was to understand the questions of revenge and forgiveness on the part of major groups after the Civil War. There were many efforts towards working for a peaceful settlement of differences regarding the slavery system. Many people did not fully comprehend the social, economical and political significance of the emancipation for blacks during the Reconstruction period. "Indeed, after several years of quasi-social and political maneuvers in the North and South, the ugliness of white supremacy arose to uncover more diabolical plans for denying equal participation in building a stronger America."

Thomas Jefferson wrote this prophetic passage concerning the mind frame of white America when he said . . . "it was found that the public mind would not bear the proposition of gradual emancipation, nor will it bear it even at this day."

Scholars strongly suggest that almost total separation between blacks and whites came after the Civil War. During this period of Reconstruction, there was a steady growth of anti-black political movements. An example of the new dogma was proclaimed by Benjamin Tillman, a southern plantation owner. "Tillman, like many others, had become a twisted, short-tempered and mean-spirited, violent politician who had sworn vengeance against the blacks."

A second political figure was Governor James K. Vardan of Mississippi. He used his influence to assure that lynching was carried on in order to maintain white supremacy. In summary, the writer quotes Governor William C. Oates of Alabama to a graduating class of Tuskegee Institute in 1884. "I want to give you niggers a few words of plain talk and advice. You might as well understand that this is a white man's country, so far as the South is concerned, and we are going to make you keep your place."

Statistics apparently proved his point. Gradually blacks were driven from the many areas of economic growth and development. Throughout the period of the late 1800's and early 1900's, most Southerners, either black or white lived a meager existence. Migration to the north was the order of the day. Positive attitudes of family unification, economic development and education were lost as both groups grappled to make an honest living and survive.

President Andrew Johnson sent his representative, Colonel Samuel Thomas to the South to observe conditions caused by the war. Colonel Thomas returned with a clear message: "I hear the people talk in such a way as to indicate that they are yet unable to conceive of black people as possessing any rights at all. Men who are honorable in their dealings with white neighbors will cheat a black without feeling a single twinge of their honor. To kill a black, they do not deem murder. The people boast that when they get freemen affairs in their own hands . . . the niggers will catch hell."

To add to the furtherance of the character assassinations of blacks after the Reconstruction period, an ever-growing negative way, the writer calls attention to the novels, songs, play, newspapers and even nursery rhymes of the day. Blacks were labeled as lazy, and playful, and were depicted as inferior to whites in all respects. During this crisis era in American history, the largest influx of Europeans were welcomed into the country. Eyes were turned to Ellis Island where Europeans came to flee persecution and economic repression. Many established white Americans reacted negatively to the arrival of the new migrants. This began a wave of propaganda and other newer weapons against their immediate merging into the society. It was not an easy period for non-whites, whether from Europe or America. New problems were created as older problems continued to concern the government of the day. The South increased its blatant and malicious position in regards to blacks, and the North tried to forget or think of blacks in compromising terms. Segregation was in order.

This was perhaps the worst period for blacks in America. Rayford Logan referred to it as "the Nadir". The South's plan against blacks cut into practically every social and economic area. Educational funds for the education of blacks were almost non-existent, as it was significant for whites.

All energies were pressed into establishing lines of demarcation in all areas of life.

For example, the familiar scenarios in southern cities were the clear signs and posters stating for "colored and whites". The rule was separation in the use of public facilities and accommodations. This system became widespread, and was known as "the Jim Crow" system.

VI. CONCLUSION

Racism in this country was a product of more than 300 years of systematic subordination of Indians and blacks by the white majority, plus later subordination by still other groups. It pervasively influences every single institution in our society; therefore, the writer attempted to survey and understand some of the problems confronting the major groups of America during its earlier history. It was clear throughout that blacks were considered inferior to whites. Blacks were to lack not only economic and political power, but also were without a cultural past. The differences were felt so strongly that their impact was to be carried over generation by generation into the present century.

Increasing understanding in order to root out and eliminate racism is a worthy objective for all Americans. Perhaps no other single issue in domestic affairs has more profound implications regarding America's success in achieving its own ideals, or the kinds of social changes that must be carried out to obtain them.

VII. BIBLIOGRAPHY

Bell, Phillip The Black Experience: An Annotated Bibliography
Washington, D.C., Prepared August 1988

Bernal, Martin Dr. Black Athena.
NY Adams Publishing Co., 1985.

Davis, Linwood and Janet Sims
The Ku Klux Klan: A Bibliography Compiled.
Connecticut: Greenwood Press, 1985.

Fishel, Leslie, and Quarles, Benjamin
Negro American A Documentary History.
Macmillan, 1968.

Hirsh, Carl S. The Riddles of Racism
NY Viking Press, 1972.

Kaplan Sidney The Black Presence in the Era of the American Revolution.
1770-1800
NY, Graphics, 1973.

Katz, William L. Reconstruction and National Growth 1865-2900
NY, Franklin Watts, 1974.

Logan, Rayford The Negro in American Life and Thought: The Nadir,
1877-1901
NY Dial Publishing Co., 1954.

Mydral, Gunnar An American Dilemma

Phillip Bell, Jr.

NY Harper & Row Publishing Co., 1962

C. Redding, Sanders The Game in Chains: The Dramatic History of the American Negro.
Philadelphia: Lippincott Co., 1950.

CHAPTER 2

A Survey of some origins of racial problems between blacks and whites from the 20th Century to the present.
An era of gradual change and promise.

OUTLINE

A survey of origins of racial problems between blacks and whites from the 20th Century to the present. An era of gradual change and promise.

I.   Racial Discrimination during the 1900's to the 1920's

II.   The 1920's, Black Protest: Self Determination

III.   The Black Plight during the 1930's and 1940's

IV.   The Civil Rights Movement/Leaders during the 50's and 60's

V.   Post-Integration—New Deal or Reconstruction Era Part II

VI.   Conclusion

VII.   Summary

VIII.   Bibliography

I. RACIAL DISCRIMINATION DURING THE 1900s TO THE 1920s

There were major historical events concerning racial concerns between blacks and whites to be noted throughout the earliest years of the 1900's. Several examples which this writer feels noteworthy of historical and political significance were the Supreme Court decision concerning Plessy v. Ferguson which upheld the "doctrine of separate but equal" outlining of the direction of segregation. Black leaders such as Booker T. Washington, and W. E. B. Dubois, to name just a few, came on the scene to help bring about some spiritual, intellectual, religious, and political uplifting for blacks. For example, Financier Andrew Carnegie "brought together a parcel of prominent Negro leaders, including Booker T. Washington, and W. E. B. Dubois, to discuss the advancement of the interests of the Negro race. The personal and ideological clashes between the two men were evident at the meeting, though there was general agreement that the group should press for absolute civil, political, and public equality."

During this particular era, the writer noted the dawn of the rise of self-help black organizations in America. Several of these organizations were the Niagara Movement which started in 1905, the National Association for the Advancement of Colored People in 1909, and the origin of the National Urban League in 1910. These groups basically were formed to assist in the struggle or abolishing all forms of distinctions based on race; however, there were notable differences made by various group leaders regarding the means of achieving this end. Finally, it should be stressed that the originators of these groups comprised many of the more famous black intellectual and political figures of that time. The organization and union of the masses of average working class blacks came during the early 1920's era with the building of the black church congregation and the charismatic black leadership.

Without a doubt, one of the busiest periods of codification efforts may have taken place during the Presidency of Woodrow Wilson. In 1913, "President Wilson refused to appoint a National Race Commission to study the social and economic status of Negroes, rejecting a proposal sponsored by Oswald Garrison Villard." Due to the climate of Northern covert and Southern overt behavior in political and social affairs, the Wilson Presidency stifled any effort for helping blacks raise their status, and led to a general deterioration of race relations or any hopes for the re-approachment between blacks and whites.

However, one of the single most devastating institutions implemented by the racist power structure to further enhance the destruction of the hopes for equal citizenry for blacks was the racist implied custom of keeping the purity of the white race known as amalgamation or miscegenation. This law was implemented to restrict intermarriage and cohabitation of blacks and whites. The law was strictly enforced by the racist power structure in order to maintain its notion of purity and superiority.

Although the law was strictly enforced and upheld concerning the males cohabitation with white females, the law was routinely ignored when white males raped black females, furthering the notion of white male domination and the creation of a caste system based on shades of the complexion. The reasoning behind this notion and presumed by the racist status quo was that blacks were commonly assumed to be unassimilateable. For example, racists believed the racial characteristics of blacks to be too vastly different from their own to be acceptable. Also, from a political and social aspect, the inferior image of blacks persisted in the American psyche in both black and white people in general. Basically blacks were deemed to be lacking in cultural and positive historical imagery, and assumed unable of cultural development. However, the underlying cause for the implementation of this law stemmed from the apparent reality of the inability of the creation of white-offspring from black parents. Thus the white race would cease to exist. This law was upheld primarily to preserve the genetic purity of the white race.

In order to enforce the law, strict punishment was used; many of the punishments were more gruesome than the fear of death itself. This emotional law became the struggle for white racists to maintain racial purity for economic reasons. The intensity of enforcing such laws were legitimized by the legal apparatus of the white primary, the Democratic party, as well as the violent acts of the Knights of the Ku Klux Klan party. These groups of racist shared a common pigment, and the belief in human rights, human superiority, and the black race position of inferior self-contained caste condition for all time. These groups of white people emphatically implied that based on biological possibilities, cross-breeding was considered undesirable, because it would produce an inferior type of human; the perverted assumption and stereotype that somehow the black race was a biologically inferior human species in comparison to the white human species. The rise of such a mood can be noted from the revival of the Ku Klux Klan in 1915. The Ku Klux Klan, began in Alabama and spread to Oklahoma, California, Oregon, Indiana, and Ohio. "(Membership in the organization reached four million in the 1920's.)"

At about the same time, many witnessed the 'Great Migration', a term coined to explain the migration of some two million blacks from southern states northward. This took place mainly because the industrial centers in the North offered the promise of more and better jobs, and the defensive doctrine that blacks took in order to handle the climate of overt racial hatred in the South. However, it can be noted that blacks did not generally deal with feelings or beliefs condemning 'amalgamation' on racial or biological grounds but concerned themselves with the nature of conformity, accommodation, and subtle protests.

The evidence of this pattern of accommodation and subtle protest can be seen in this description of the coping strategy of black leaders concerning the doctrine of amalgamation principle on any reason other than social accommodation. Even the more liberal-minded Northern whites or blacks from cosmopolitan cultures, with a minimum of conventional prejudices, would in nine out of ten cases, express a definite feeling against amalgamation. This attitude of refusing to consider amalgamation, felt and expressed in the entire country, constituted the center in the complex of attitudes which might be described as the "common denominator" in the attitudes of the subtle form of black protest. In conjunction with this development of subtle protest was the development of the black church. The voice of allowable dissension had generally come from the pulpit through the years. During this stage the black church had become the instrument for black unity and protest.

Throughout the early 1900's, the racist power-base had seemingly been aware of protest from the church environment; however, generally they viewed this effort of denunciation of white oppression as a tolerable form of passive protest. Yet it was during this era of the great black retreat, that the black pulpit had become the primary political foundation for black socioeconomic development. Example of gradual development can be seen in the various areas; the mastery of the bible became an instrument of psychological and educational awakening. Throughout the era, the black clergy evolved into leaders for negotiating the status-quo power-base for the black race. The black church became the major social organization for the masses regarding the social, political, and economic development.

II. THE 1920'S, BLACK PROTEST: SELF DETERMINATION

Throughout the international community, the United States of America had become known as a society based on racial quotas; "hypocrisy disguised as Democracy" in regards to the black race. The political reality of declaring the creed of white supremacy within the democratic creed, author and editorialist William Allan White sums up the political ambition of white supremacists perhaps the best; "It is the Anglo-Saxon manifest destiny to go forth in the world as a world conqueror. He will take possession of all islands of the seas. He will exterminate the peoples he cannot subjugate. That is what fate holds for the chosen people. It is so written. Those who would protest found their objectives overruled."

In conjunction with the fervor of white supremacy and the powerful unification of white supremacist groups, it can also be noted as a time of increased radical efforts to improve the socioeconomic conditions for the masses of blacks. This era was basically the origin of black protest; self-determination in the expression often termed as Black Nationalism. One such figure who came to prominence as the symbol of militancy, and nonconformity, was Marcus Garvey, a Jamaican born black who came to America, and was successful in arousing the consciousness of the masses of blacks unlike any before or since his time. Because he viewed the situation for civil and human justice in America as hopeless, Garvey's goal was to promote the idea that black Americans should leave America, and to return to the Mother continent of its cultural origin. Marcus Garvey possessed the ability to organize and mobilize the masses of blacks in a political body in 1920. For example, Garvey opened "The National Convention of the Universal Negro Improvement Association", and raised millions of dollars to start a shipping company as well as other black owned ventures.

III. THE BLACK PLIGHT DURING THE 1930'S AND 1940'S

The statement by the late author, James Weldon Johnson, can be noted as a more relevant statement regarding this era concerning blacks in America. He stated, "He or she is forced to take his outlook on all things, not from the viewpoint of a colored man. It is wonderful to me that the race has progressed so broadly as it has, since most of its thoughts and all of its activities must run through the narrow neck of this one funnel."

Black people, despite segregation and racism, had managed to contribute to the advancement of the race and American society in many areas of life. Blacks were maturing from their participation in the war effort and Olympic competitions, and were liberating themselves gradually from the image of inferior beings. Blacks such as Jessie Owens and Joe Louis, had a significant impression on the progress and motivation for achievement in the mainstream of American life. Also those black American men and women who served abroad during the war effort would not forget the freedoms experienced overseas nor remain in a mind frame of passive, helpless, and inferior beings. From their military experience blacks found new feelings of equality that can be traced to this specific stage of socioeconomic development in black American history. The following quotes highlight the major contributions of Black Americans who managed to achieve prominence nationally and internationally although the climate of America was that of segregation. "Jesse Owens wins four gold medals in the 1936 Olympics." "In 1938 Crystal Bird Fauset of Philadelphia, the first Negro woman Legislator, was elected to the Pennsylvania House of Representatives." Also in 1940, "The appointment of Benjamin O. Davis, Sr. the first Negro General in the History of the Armed Forces."

These blacks and many others made tremendous gains despite the many political and social pressures staged by whites to ensure that the black masses were kept from the mainstream of social and economic development. Many blacks were charged with sedition for speaking out on issues regarding American policies relative to their life. The intimidation tactics to keep blacks from the polls were both political and physical in nature. However, it can also be seen that this era marked the advancement of blacks, a momentous stage that was highlighted by significant political rulings that improved the civil rights of blacks in the laws of the land. One such example of change in American laws affecting blacks can be noted in the following statement, "The Truman Committee on Civil Rights formally condemned racial injustice in the widely quoted report 'To Secure These Rights'."

IV. THE CIVIL RIGHTS MOVEMENT/ LEADERS DURING THE 50'S AND 60'S

It can be argued that the mood of America really began to turn drastically regarding the absolute civil, political, and public equality for blacks; in conjunction with the forces of militancy, non-violent protest, legal and political figures. A social phenomenon took place in America that can be assessed as the first 'Bloodless Revolution' in history. This was the period in history for blacks when segregation ended with the refusal of a black woman named Rosa Parks to leave her seat on a Montgomery Alabama bus, because of an Alabama law stating that the blacks must give their seats to white riders. This incident sparked a 382-day bus boycott, and also gave rise to the prominence of one of the world's greatest social reformers, Dr. Martin Luther King, Jr. A 27-year old minister from Georgia, Dr. King coordinated this protest, and as a result became the most influential spokesperson for the masses of blacks since the time of Marcus Garvey.

This era was highlighted by major demonstrations which ranged from the integration efforts of black students in places such as: Little Rock's Central High School, the University of Alabama, and University of Mississippi; to sit-ins, marches, and riots in major American cities such as: Watts, Chicago, Jackson, Selma, and Montgomery. So these early years of integration could be seen as the union of several areas of black leadership such as: clergymen like Dr. Martin Luther Kings, Jr., lawyers, like Thurgood Marshall, and civil right activists such as Malcolm X and Medgar Evers. These men and many others helped to bring about justice regarding civil rights in America.

Unlike any other time in America, intense violence and unrest between blacks and whites marred this era. Many of the champions of the civil rights movement were assassinated. Men such as Dr. King, Malcolm X, Medgar Evers, President John F. Kennedy, and Senator Robert Kennedy were the more notable figures involved politically and socially in the civil rights movement. These men were murdered because of their fight for social change. These American leaders, as political and social reformers helped push social forces to correct America's three centuries of injustice and inequality concerning blacks in America in the span of roughly 20 years. Unlike the era of Reconstruction, the full union of all social and political forces, in addition to medial exposure of racial injustices helped to truly ensure permanence to segregation and legal oppression of blacks in America.

Also significant to note, the lack of these civil rights and the unification to obtain them, would also be the catalyst to the underlying tide of essence among other disenfranchised populations, such as the anti-Vietnam War protesters, Women's Liberation Movement, and Environmentalists. It gave rise to the power of unity, demonstration, and media exposure regarding the means of social change. This era can be assessed as the point in American history that several oppressed groups spearheaded by the push of the black movement all cashed in on the opportunity for social reform including human rights. For blacks it meant the potential opportunity had finally come to move freely throughout the mainstream of American society without the Jim Crow restrictions so prevalent throughout the first 60 years of the 1900's.

However, it should be noted that the expectations for a quick transformation of power, and the smooth transition into these new found opportunities cannot be seen in retrospect concerning the Era of Reconstruction after the Emancipation Proclamation. However, it can be seen perhaps in the psychological mood of both blacks and whites concerning these newfound liberties. So not only would the changing of the American laws be necessary, but also a change in the psychological mood of both races—especially whites. The deepness of the problem concerning blacks in the areas of psychological adjustment from past ostracizes, and white backlash during the era would be the major problem the writer will attempt to bring into focus during the era of integration/post-integration.

V. POST-INTEGRATION - NEW DEAL OR RECONSTRUCTION ERA PART II

"This lack of power generally causes a sense of despair, a sense of hopelessness that nothing will change, and a negative perception of self and other Negroes; due to the psychological problems of over three and a half centuries. At this point, the suppressed protest throughout the past centuries will be taking new forms of overt expression and in many cases, negative actions of expressions against other blacks and society in general."

The prophetic statement regarding the current social dilemma that is evident concerning American society in general reflects the racial problems from America's past in regards to the effect of the black and white learned negative behaviors. These negative disorders manifests itself in the perpetuate of self-defeating behaviors, and whites social and political manipulation regarding the destruction of black socioeconomic development.

Although the plight of the Afro-American concerning its attainment of full social and economic rights in America should become a possible reality given the examples of other cultural and ethnic groups attempt in becoming successful in America's 'melting pot'; however the dilemma persist in how blacks can work out this transformation of equality just like other groups have as naturally as possible. Specifically to work out this transformation into the technological age with its economic, educational, and social sophistication's in lieu of the traditional scenario of blacks being left out of the socioeconomic mainstream of centuries past.

The scenario described above shed illumination on the evolution of the sociological and psychological dilemma that black's face in spite of the unnatural perception of blacks and the historical disfranchisement from the socioeconomic system afforded all whites and basically all other minorities who came to America voluntarily. The reality of this scenario points out the distorted and biased perception of the status-quo concerning realistically understanding and addressing the transformation process given the cultural rapping of blacks during three and a half centuries in America. According to various authorities, such as, Gunnar Myrdal, Thomas Sowell, Malcolm X, William Ryan, and Early Conrad, they all seemed in agreement that the white power structure intends to direct their plan and not the plan of black leadership in regards to the transformation process to rectify the wrongs of the past. However, they do not, or they cannot, fully understand the psychological dynamics wholeheartedly, and share in the vision of truly correcting the ills concerning the masses of blacks. The reasoning behind this is the overall cost and division of power. This shift in the white power structure to suddenly allow so many who were traditionally used as a means to obtain the white imbalance of wealth and power in America would cause a true revolution in the socioeconomic fabric of the status-quo. And the status quo is not, and will not tolerate a loss in comfort and wealth.

This scenario, whether conscious or unconscious is the reality of the continual psychological, sociological, and economic disfranchisement of the masses of blacks. Then based on this premise, the socioeconomic status of the masses of blacks in relation to the white power structure will continue to exist as it has generally existed before integration. That is basically what the system is presently, a perpetuation; during the age of technology of the "Master Race - Servant Race" relationship. The reality of the structure regardless of the infusion of cultures into the mainstream of America's socioeconomic mainstream still depicts the "Peculiar Institution' discrimination against black Americans. It is prevailing norm and will in all probability continue for years to come. According to many, integration is seen as just a newer oppressive system that has updated methods of achieving the same goals as achieved in the past centuries. Also noted, many share the notion that the transformation for the masses of blacks may have forever destroyed the possibility for a natural transformation. According to this passage from Gunnar Myrdal's 'An American Dilemma' the writer translated this statement regarding the realization of transformation during integration. "The way defeatism works in destroying the achievement levels of blacks today in conjunction with overt and covert actions of the white power-base has caused an internal war among the classes and the masses of blacks. Therefore, creating a grander problem of racial bigotry, which could prove to be far more dangerous and far more advantageous to the permanence of the status quo." Thus black people often view this analogy in general as the status-quo's genocidal plan which attempts to break the will power and basically return the masses of blacks to a caste of second class citizenry in our present era. This will ensure that the power structure will not be financially burdened with an institution, which it created; yet viewed as a low priority because of cost and its negative perception of the black human life.

According to author William Ryan, this quoted passage further explains the current ideological viewpoint of the white power structure ammunition and low prioritizing of black human life. Ryan states, "The generic formula of 'Blaming the Victim'—justifying the inequality by finding defects in the victims of inequality—has been retained, but in a much wider, more malevolent and dangerous form, particularly in the resurgence of ideas about hereditary defects in blacks, the poor, and working people in general." In a broader analogy, the writer and Ryan observe that the correct sociological explanation concerning black failures to assimilate wholesale into the mainstream of American society stems from the race's biological inferiority to Whites. The status quo creates the illusion that the mere passing of civil right laws within the last twenty years has given total rise to the economic and social development of the masses of blacks if they are genetically capable.

In essence the plan by whites works; that new civil laws, jobs, and social freedoms that were totally denied thus suddenly blankets over the psychosocial vestiges of racism from both blacks and whites. The vestiges of hurt, mistrust, identity, poverty, and social upheaval for blacks, and in regards to whites, the feelings of apathy, revenge, superiority, and economic restructuring of its status quo. According to this plan, if the black race does not respond normally, then it must be truth to the premise of genetic inferiority, and permanence of the justification of the 'master race'—slave race system, that is so prevalent in the American psychosocial subconscious. Then the plan of the white owned-structure has always been a social and political farce to give the same attention to blacks thus the current failure of the masses of blacks to rise out of their economic condition can be viewed socioeconomically as irreversible. If the status-quo's plan is to leave out causes and effects of the socioeconomic conditions to America's people, all races will be kept ignorant; thus, what will be the effect on future relationships of races in America? What will the socioeconomic conditions of the masses of blacks be like? And finally what strategies will the white power structure develop in order to handle the psychosocial dilemmas of defeatism, which is so prevalent during this era of integration-post-integration.

34

VI. CONCLUSION

Therefore, in regards to writer's research and observations from job-related experiences and theoretical viewpoints expressed by authors and intellectuals noted in writer's bibliography; the prophetic conclusion which can be drawn from writers' literary survey can be noted. The current strategy of stimulating the socioeconomic development of blacks can be viewed as a plan of psychosocial neglect. That blacks are the blame for their own failures, and that the rise of 'Uncle Tomism' a way that blacks who are making it handle their socioeconomic inferiority, and ultimately, it can be viewed as a way out of guilt through disassociation.

Therefore, the black problem will be used as an economy booster, an internal war effort, by allowing the terrorism and violence by blacks among blacks and against blacks, to continue to escalate to the levels so high that all races will cry out for government intervention regarding the social maladaptive behaviors of the ignorant and misguided blacks selling and taking illicit drugs. A problem basically due to the psychosocial and economic deficiencies perpetuated by the racist white power structure. New jobs will be created in areas such as law enforcement, weapon's manufacturing, prison construction, legal and social welfare reformers who all help to maintain order, which continues the permanence of the racist white power structure and the status quo.

Finally, the writer will note this hypothetical scenario which some see as currently evolving and others as a possibility if current programs do not work. The urban cities become an unmanageable breeding ground for social unrest and crime. The governments both state and local are forced to react in order to restore normalcy at any cost. The existing social agents, such as the judges, lawyers, social workers, policemen, weapons manufacturers, and prison construction developers will all be stimulated economically due to the demand for their services. The beginnings of this scenario, whether viewed as a genocidal plan or not, can be seen regarding present day problems. The status-quo's response has basically been that of reactive methods and strategies, versus the more pro-active methods often voiced by blacks and socially progressive leaders knowledgeable in the areas of human psycho-social matters.

VII. SUMMARY

The American creed concerning Black Americans in general can be seen as a mythological creed regarding its image as a nation built on the premise of hard work, fairness, and integrity, which are the characteristics that were ironically unnatural to Black Americans. Therefore, given America's historical case study can it attempt to be a true moral leader in regards to democracy when in practice; it is seen as just a myth specific to a few, and detrimental to many specifically Black Americans.

The reality of America's mistreatment of blacks regarding its democratic creed is two-fold. First, it has potentially sentenced a race of people to a man-made hell beside a man-made heaven and second, its injustices against blacks has potentially stifled the living moral and economic soul from a nation endowed with vast amounts of economic and human resources. The fallout from America's hypocritical myth concerning blacks specifically is that of a picture that is painted as a nation with just a formula for freedom and creativity prostituting its creed and democracy for the dollars and wealth at the expense of others. This usury image unless truly corrected, will bring upon itself the curses, which befall the users with time.

This literary summary is an attempt to address the subtle psycho-social vestiges of White racism and the present issues being played out in order for the white power-structure to maintain the status-quo in the basic areas of the American socioeconomic process. There is no doubt that racism exists in the American institution today; however, unlike ever before, many concerned humanitarians are working toward a true revolution to drive the masses and attain full socioeconomic justice and positive long-term relationship between the races.

BIBLIOGRAPHY

Bell, Phillip. The Black Experience an Annotated Bibliography
Washington, D.C., Prepared August 1988

Conrad, Earl. The Invention of the Negro
New York: Harper & Row Publishing Co., 1962

Mydral, Gunner. An American Dilemma
NY Harper & Row Publishing Co., 1962

Ploski, Harry A. & Kaiser, Ernest.
The Negro Almanac
New York: The Belwether Co., 1971

Ryan, William. Blaming the Victim
New York: Vintage Books, 1976

CHAPTER 3

Historical Commentary Focusing on Racial Problems in America from the 17th Century to the Present 21st Century Plantation Conspiracy

OUTLINE

Historical commentary focusing on racial problems in America from the 19th Century to the present

I. Introduction
II. A General Historical Commentary Summary on the Focus of Black Achievements
    A. 1865 - 1875 (Reconstruction)
    B. 1886 - 1900
    C. 1901 - 1929
    D. 1930 - Present
III. 2000 Forecast
IV. Conclusion

I. INTRODUCTION

Man's quest for justice. This struggle to overcome social injustices, religious intolerance, racial discrimination and segregation did not begin in 20th Century United States. Actually from ancient times to the present, the struggle for rights has been the cause of countless social and political conflicts and will continue to be.

The Founding Fathers knew that slavery was a mocking of human rights. The two systems could not exist side by side. From time to time many interpreted the Constitution for their own purposes and America became a segregated nation. The struggle grew and developed into a larger conflict. States argued against states over the issue of cheap labor and the status of people of color. The climax came with Civil War, 1860 and ended with the signing of the Treaty at Appomatox Court House.

This study however, concentrates on the period after the war.

II. A GENERAL HISTORICAL COMMENTARY SUMMARY ON THE FOCUS OF BLACK ACHIEVEMENTS

A. 1865 - 1875 (Reconstruction)

It was April 9, 1865 at Appomatox Court House that Robert E. Lee surrendered to Ulysses E. Grant. The Civil War meant the fall of King Cotton and the old way of life. Hopes were cherished for freedom, education and guaranteed rights, although most of the freed men had no education, no money, no employment and also no place to live. Proud Southerners refused to accept freed men as citizens and began to rebuild with fierce determination bitterly opposing any changes.

Responsible leaders recognized the fact that freedmen needed adjustment and between 1865 and 1875 the United States government passed laws to provide and protect the rights of all free people. Except for a brief period, minorities and blacks never really experienced freedom and justice as guaranteed by the Constitution. "White Supremacy" became the rallying cry and 'states rights' became the political menus used to pass and uphold unjust laws. There was a basic struggle between states rights and the authority of the central government.

President Abraham Lincoln pushed for strong national legislation's regarding the freedmen. Congress passed and the states ratified the Thirteenth, Fourteenth, and Fifteenth Amendments. The Freedmen's Bureau was established to help make the transition from bondage to freedom easier. The Southern states answered with state laws called the 'black codes'.

The black codes, boldly passed by several southern states were designed to impede the social, political and economic progress of former slaves. These codes involved work requirements, interracial marriages, vagrancy, owning and renting land.

These were not genuine attempts to rebuild the South and to assist the former slaves in beginning their lives as free people. While legislators were writing laws to protect the rights of all citizens; the laws were no more than "paper rights".

During this period of Reconstruction schools, churches, and small businesses were struggling to gain a foothold. Over a dozen black colleges and manual trade institutions were founded: Hampton Institute in Virginia; Morehouse in Georgia; Howard in Washington; and Fisk in Tennessee. However, just as it was difficult for the black office holder, it was worse for the voter. When intimidation, deceit and threats did not work, violence became the order of the day, just as the Civil Rights Act of 1875, to protect all citizens in their civil and legal rights—were enacted, gentlemen Southerners were merchants, farmers, businessmen during the day but invisible hoodsmen riding throughout the countryside at night taking the law into their own hands.

B. 1886 - 1900

Historians mark the 1876 election year as the unofficial end of Reconstruction. Attitudes had slightly changed and younger leaders were more willing to compromise. Even though thirty-five states were seated in Congress, 1876 was hailed as having the most disgraceful, corrupt election of all times. Ballot boxes were destroyed; houses were burned, military troops were attacked and hooded Klansmen drove blacks from voting places. Clearly the bargain for Hayes to become president ended the period in reconstruction. Black hopes were shattered as President Hayes refused to accept reports of terror, voting violations, beatings, burnings, and lynching. Hayes turned his attention to industrialization and international recognition of the country as an industrial power.

America celebrated its hundredth birthday in 1876. Philadelphia hosted the Centennial Exposition. Inventions were on display; the sewing machine changed the clothing industry, railroads replaced river transportation, wagon trains left for the Southwest. Thousands of Europeans and Asians left their homelands for a new way of life. Many blacks settled in Arkansas, Louisiana and Texas, while others found jobs in factories and mills. Even though housing and educational opportunities were minimal, blacks felt more privileged in the urban areas then ever before.

In the 1800's, over 23.5 million foreigners entered the United States and settled along the eastern sea cost. Sixty percent of those immigrants were peasants from Italy, Russia, Austria, Hungary, Bulgaria, Turkey, Poland and Greece. They were fleeing from religious and political persecution. Eastern cities were bulging. Illiteracy was high and incomes were low. Young children took jobs in mines and sweatshops. Neighborhoods turned into slums, crime spread and racial prejudice provided a comfortable scapegoat.

It was not a comfortable time elsewhere in the United States. The Chinese were experiencing racism on the West Coast. There were violent race riots and the Chinese worker was the victim. The Japanese experienced similar limitations based solely on racism. In the Southwest, Mexican-Americans disregarded borderlines and settled on the states. Some were tolerated for the cheap labor; others were victimized. Indians were stereotyped as noble savages or murderous heathens. Through trickery, they lost their homelands and freedom, being forced to live on reservations.

Meanwhile, debates over voting rights were underway. Women gained support for the suffrage; black men were losing vital support for theirs. According to statistics compiled by Ida B. Wells Barnett, blacks were being lynched on the average of two per week throughout the south.

Blacks quickly learned that the only way to make their dreams come true was to wake up to the harsh realities and fight back. Black leadership chose education as a weapon and the press was a positive strategy.

By 1900, there were about 150 weekly black newspapers published. The Pittsburgh Courier, Chicago Defender and St. Louis Argus were examples of quality newspapers, which played "key roles in advancing the levels of the races' knowledge, pride and militancy".

Black leaders began to organize so that they might present a unified front when negotiating with state and federal administrations. The National Convention of Colored People was held in 1883, in Louisville, Kentucky. The National Baptist Convention and the National Baptist Publishing House were started at this time.

The major point of concern was racism. Race prejudice was no longer contained in the South; it was spreading to points North and West. The trend toward segregation—a forced separation of the races—was growing all over the country. The National Negro Convention adopted a Constitution and formed a League oriented toward a high redress of grievances. It was the forerunner of the National Association for the Advancement of Colored People (NAACP). By the end of the century, the first generation of freeborn blacks was performing as skilled workers, college graduates and responsible citizens. Yet all the great strides made during the period were reversing. Here was one step forward and with the Plessy vs. Ferguson decision, two steps back.

C: 1901 – 1929

By 1900, segregation had become an acceptable social system that was instituted by various state laws and upheld by the Supreme Court. The south was rigidly segregated; two communities existed side by side, separate and very unequal.

The race issues was not of primary concern to politicians in the early 1900's. America was rapidly becoming a world power and 'a champion of democracy'. Leaders, somehow, were able to justify the existence of segregation in a democratic society by stressing that point that races were separate but equal. This position was later to become an embarrassment when criticizing the human rights policies of other countries.

The period between 1900 and 1920 known as the Great Migration peaked just before World War I. Thousands entered the United States through Ellis Island where facilities were established to screen all newcomers. There were no quotas placed on the number who could enter. By 1929, the immigration wave had ceased. An American multicultural society was created bringing with it its food, clothing, language ideas, and customs that were changed forever.

As the immigrants (white) became citizens, they were automatically given full rights of citizenship with the right to vote, hold office, own property, borrow money and begin businesses using the opportunities available, they lifted themselves out of poverty. This was not easy for Black Americans.

Angered by the acceptance of newly arriving immigrants, blacks made a vain attempt to assimilate but this was not to be an easy task. Myths and stereotypes were created out of ignorance. History books did not include the contribution of minorities and facts were often distorted or ignored.

Carter G. Woodson, a militant of his time, set out to preserve black history and record it accurately. He wrote several volumes and organized the Association for the Study of Negro Life and History in 1915. In 1926, Woodson introduced Negro History Week, now celebrated during the entire month of February.

The Roaring Twenties came to a halt in 1929. The stock market crashed and the bottom fell out of the American economy. In 1932, the Nation elected President Franklin D. Roosevelt. Roosevelt began his economic recovery program called the New Deal. He set into motion such projects as the National Recovery Administration (NRA), the Civilian Conservation Corps (CCC), the Agricultural Adjustment Administration (AAA), and the Works Progress Administration (WPA).

D. 1930 – Present

By 1938, Europe was at war while employment opportunities for blacks remained limited. On December 7, 1941, Japanese aircraft attacked the American fleet at Pearl Harbor. Time passed and on August 6, 1945, a B-29 bomber dropped the first atomic bomb on Hiroshima and another on Nagasaki three days later. The War was over but the peace was not secure.

The appointment of the Civil Rights Commission was formed and outlined some recommendations for President Harry Truman to consider. Some of the proposals were not put into effect, however much of the legislation passed between 1957 and 1975 used the report as a model.

School desegregation was the major domestic political issue between 1955 and 1960. Some school districts quietly integrated and transitions were made without major incidents. In the Deep South, while leadership encouraged their people to resist, there were endless rounds of debates and assignments. When this failed, force and violence were used to obstruct justice.

However, the momentum seemed to be moving in favor of blacks. Public opinion was shifting towards more liberal civil rights legislation. The Civil Rights Act of 1957 called for the establishment of a special Civil

Rights Division and the creation of a Federal Civil Rights Commission to study the status of civil rights in the nation.

It was too late to turn back the hands of time. When nine black students arrived at Central high school, Arkansas protestors surrounded it. This incident was met with a forceful response. Paratroopers and troops of the 101st Airborne Division escorted the group on campus.

Rosa Parks decided to remain seated and was fined fourteen dollars because of her protest. The Montgomery Bus Boycott was a response to the situation and had a definite effect on the downtown trades. The movement continued during the administration of President John F. Kennedy and his brother Attorney General Robert F. Kennedy.

With the Kennedy administration giving support, the movement grew ever stronger and bold Black leaders planned a march on Washington, August 28, 1963; to coincide with the anniversary of the Emancipation Proclamation which was signed in 1863. The march was an unforgettable event. W.E.B. DuBois passed away in Ghana, at the age of ninety-five. It was the end of an era.

Progress still had its downside, not all the events in the Civil rights struggle were pleasant and inspiring. There were to follow church bombings, assassinations and riots. Minorities were becoming more aware of themselves and of their potentials. Black history materials were primarily inaccurate, insensitive and inadequate. Although schools were integrated textbooks excluded the contributions of blacks, women and other minorities. Through persistence, schools were convinced the multi-cultural education was the best approach. This process took years to implement and in fact, the effort continues today.

This was the true beginning of new and rich experiences for blacks. As they moved together, they showed a greater maturity as a result of past experiences. Blacks are, and continue to be an integral part of the western culture and civilization.

Africans being taken to European slave traders.

Africans loaded on a slave ship.

Slave auction in New Orleans in the 1950s

Slaves in a cotton field

Nat Turner stages an uprising against slave owners.

Harriet Tubman (left) and some people she helped.

Dred Scott

Harriet Scott

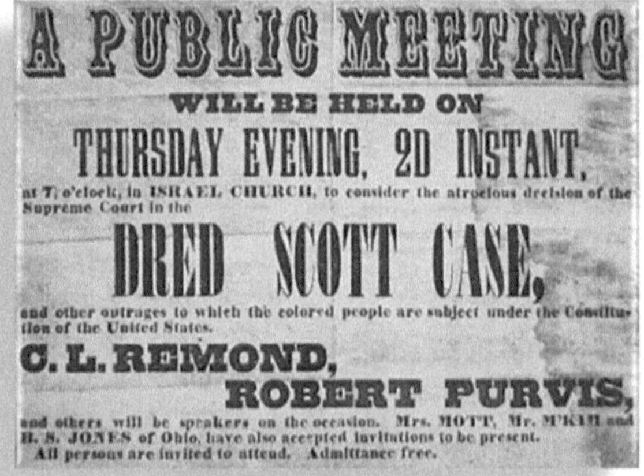

Dred Scott proclamation public meeting

Soldiers of the 4TH U. S. Colored Infantry.

Abraham Lincoln

George B. McClellan

George B. McClellan

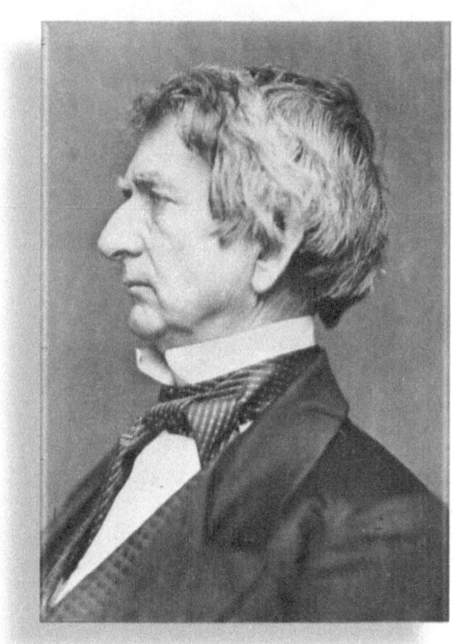

William H. Seward

Frederick Douglass

Booker T. Washington

W. E. B. Du Bois

Sojourner Truth

Harriet Tubman

Honorable Marcus Mosiah Garvey

Malcolm X

Dr. Martin Luther King, Jr.

Rosa Parks

Jesse Jackson

Elizabeth Eckford integrates her high school

Students in Florida being bused to school

Ku Klux Klan march

Black Panther Leader Huey Newton speaking in Philadelphia

African Americans gather to protest in Washington, D.C.

Civil Rights Marchers assemble at the State Capitol in Montgomery, Alabama

Jackie Robinson

Muhammad Ali

**1968 Olympic Games Black
Power Salute**

III. 2000 Forecast

The 21st Century
American Plantation
Plantation System, Race in America - 21st Century
The Courts, Jails & Police

"I recommend fair and equal punishment. Children should not abuse their youth and bodies; however, parents must work to improve parenting responsibilities and skills to produce such realistically. An oppressive society can be marked by suppressive dysfunctional behavior. Many people in control and our social infrastructures have and do manifest such abusive and destructive practices".

This text is a compilation of historical and contemporary social commentaries of research designed to help enlighten and possibly give some spiritual direction to the negative problems facing our country and the world.

Prejudices are felt by all in some way—gender, faith, culture, economics, race and others. However, this text focuses on legacy of race past and present and hope to give a succinct, yet thorough and action provoking account.

The American Plantain 21st Century

Today, in the year 2000, it is considered to be politically correct to admit America's historic legacy of injustice concerning race. Race problems are not unique regarding the history of mankind. However, the truth of history must be recorded for present and future generations in order to stimulate change for a healthy and more productive society. Racism has been and still is a cancer in America's society. In the Plantation 21st Century chapter, I will enhance a positive dialogue regarding race relations. The negative legacy of race hatred and race dominance has left its mark on the American scene. The destructive process of the American race hatred legacy has presently manifested itself in unfair practices and social distinctions; thereby re-establishing control under the disguise law and legal practices. The disproportionate arrests of blacks and minorities are well documented. American men and women serving time in jail for non-violent and non-property issues are overwhelmingly black and poor. An increase of innocent people being harassed and their constitutional rights being violated such as the planting of evidence and the stopping of motorist for no probable causes are examples of race hatred through legal devices.

The plantation 21st Century appears to be the trappings of jails, prisons, IRS, FBI, the American drug agenda, drug cartels, the pervasive ideologies of racism, and ignorance imbedded into the hearts of its people. For example crack cocaine is slavery. The dealers and the police are slave overseers, the drug lords are the slave traders, and the politicians are the plantation owners. It is well documented that in the 60's J. Edgar Hoover, the Mafia drug cartels, and men of no conscience developed a plan to destroy the youth and positive social mobility of America's Black population. Now that the facts are well-documented about Hoover's paranoia and conspiracy against Black Americans. This may prove to is the worst modern day crime regarding the American racial legacy.

House Judiciary Committee Hearing on Police Misconduct
House of Representatives
Case Study: Volousia County, Florida
Through Brunswick, Georgia

This case is based on an actual event. The names of those involved have been changed. On October 29, 1999, 7:00 p.m. several Brunswick County troopers falsely accuse a Black man of trafficking drugs on the 95 North Highway. Two days prior to the drug arrest, Mr. John Dell watched a television documentary on police misconduct and abuse of power near the area where he was vacationing. In the program, men and women abused by police offered information and advice on the current trends of abuse of blacks, particularly black men, on our nation's highways.

Mr. Dell, a 36 year old, God-fearing, health conscious spiritual, self-employed individual who had never been arrested for any crime in his life, had no idea of what he was about to experience. Driving a red rent-a-car, on his return trip from vacation in Florida, Mr. Dell arrived in Brunswick County, Georgia. Stopping for food and fuel, Mr. Dell sat outside his car waiting for his passenger and friend to come out of a convenience store. He casually noticed a trooper's car pass by, he thought nothing of it. Mr. Dell and his passenger left the convenience store and continued on their trip. A quarter of a mile down the road they noticed the trooper had pulled over to the shoulder. To their surprise, the trooper turned on his lights and sirens to pull them over. The trooper was quickly joined by two other police cars. Confident that he had not committed any traffic offenses, Mr. Dell considered this to be unusual behavior. Recalling the C-Span program on racism on American highways, he realized that he might now be a victim of the same experience described on the documentary.

The troopers approached him with what is believed to be fabricated story, of a tip they received that his car was involved in trafficking drugs. Knowing that he was not a drug trafficker, the fear and disappointment that came over him and his companion was overwhelmingly stressful. He unfortunately realized that he, like others, was being set up for trafficking drugs. The troopers wanted to search his vehicle, but Mr. Dell refused because of fears that they would plant a substance to substantiate their charge. However the police managed to harass Mr. Dell into allowing a car search. Mr. Dell finally agreed to allow the dogs to search his vehicle believing the dogs were trustworthy.

The dog began to search the bumper of the car and the ground near the bumper, making Mr. Dell agree to allow the police to search the vehicle. There they uncovered his companion's medicinal amount of marijuana, which may have amounted to 1 marijuana cigarette, the troopers told him that under normal circumstances if he had allowed them to search the car initially, without the dogs, the amount would have been thrown into the dirt. Mr. Dell also had another problem. His companion, who was on a number of different medications, now seemed to be having a mild heart attack due to the high level of excitement and close quarters of the squad car. Mr. Dell was forced to make the decision to accept the responsibility for the marijuana because his companion did not appear to be able to endure the arrest procedure and lacked legal assistance resources. Therefore, Mr. Dell was arrested by the troopers and taken to Brunswick County jail.

Mr. Dell and his companion found themselves in a strange city, handcuffed in the back of a police car and taken to the county jail. The process of posting bond was further complicated by the fact that they had no nearby relatives or friends. Mr. Dell's companion tried throughout the night to raise the $726 needed for bond. The arresting officer had forgotten to give Mr. Dell his wallet back. Without his wallet, Mr. Dell did not have access to information needed to contact his attorney. Therefore he spent 18 hours in jail until his family made bail. This case was dropped due to the work of his attorney. However, Mr. Dell's companion was so distraught over the incident that her private doctor informed her that she had suffered a mild heart attack. Mr. Dell reports never feeling quite comfortable around police officers. He believes that the treatment that he received from Brunswick police was a reflection of many other racists in America. He is unsure whom to trust and fears ending up a victim of racism again. Mr. Dell questions the progress this country has made in race relations.

Some think that police brutality today is reminiscent of the overseers and slave-breakers on plantations during the days of slavery. On the 21st Century American Plantation slaves can be seen as workers who supply labor and services and those in authority over workers having the power to violate incarcerate and possibly kill those subject to them. Many activists openly advocate a return to the violence for violence approach of other eras to rectify issues of inequity of the Plantation 21st Century. Historically, violence has not worked and will also prove to be ineffective at this time. The truth is that violence has had its place in social change historically, but so has non-violence. How do we begin to change things? We must wage an all out war on ignorance, hate, as well as violence. At no other time in American history has this type of war been waged since Dr. King had his dream. It is now time to move towards the full realization through following a method and plan.

We can all understand the anger and frustration of some Americans when it comes to excessive governmental control, unfair practices, high taxation, corrupt legislators and police. Those subject to these injustices are incited to challenge their offenders militarily or mutiny. Shifting the balance of power to those who have more weapons used for conflict moves the oppressor towards the next step; forced suicide and genocide.

Idealistically the system would work better if people knew the truth in advance concerning very real life boundaries, opportunities, health, and welfare in our nation.

Realistically we don't have that in our current system. At best, it would have taken several years longer than the urgent issues of decades of prejudice that have been in place throughout America for the past 320 years. It did not just start with Hoover, the Drug Cartel, and other covert and overt conspirators that wanted to destroy men for reasons of race or greed. Include the many that didn't and don't come to action, because they are programmed to believe that America has no problem with prejudice. They are the same generally who can't discern other immediate issues, such as global warming and the vast AIDS epidemic. Therefore, if we are to prevent the development of America's 21st Century Plantation System we must step out of a complacency mode and begin to develop a mind set for the long haul regarding the re-education of our society.

Are we all on the 21st Century Plantation now?

Although many of you have not personally been touched in some way by the process of unfair seizure and probably cannot relate yet, beware, this is not a paranoid conspiracy theory. American race profiling is a reality. "Big Brother" is watching you!

If we look at the current system of law enforcement, seventy percent of people incarcerated are there for drugs. However, the flow and desire for drugs remain. It would appear that incarcerating people for non-violent crimes and placing them among violent criminals would produce more serious behavior problems. It would compare to placing a STD patient in a ward with AIDS patients and using the same needle. One does not have to be a rocket scientist to see the outcome as well as the psychological and personal damage done. You are telling society that if a politician is intelligent enough to run a major state and possibly a country but has admitted to using cocaine as a youth. Does this make him any less qualified? Probably not, however, there are many people rotting away behind bars for something they may have done like this politician but may not have had the ways of evading the system which unfairly seeks out and profiles a segment of the American population.

The African-American population has been estimated at around 13 percent of the American population. However, they make up well over

50 percent of the American prison population. Hispanics and the poor generally make up the other remaining percentage. Now if we were to use the European model of handling our drug epidemic, I think that we would be well on our way of reducing race-related prejudice in this country. We could use the resources toward rehabilitation rather than the Puritan Euro-American method of harsh punishment and repentance.

Ask yourself the next time you see someone arrested for drug possession what it would be like if you were arrested every time you drank a beer or smoked a cigarette. Then ask yourself what it would be like to suffer a stronger punishment because you were a woman, or had blond hair or slanted eyes. How irrational a solution would this be? And think about it, if you were placed in a jail until you could raise your bond or prove your innocence. Also remember that seventy percent of these minor offenders are placed into an environment where one-out-of-three might suffer bodily harm or even a perverted act. Think about the life you would lead and the feelings you would have day-to-day in your attempt to survive.

America has had a legacy of profiting off the blacks and other minorities in her past, although, the system was much more overt in practice. Nonetheless, today in America, a more sinister conspiracy although much more covert in practice has produced an environment that can be compared to the plantation system. In America, the plantation was an all black enslaved population on large tracks of land generally treated like beasts of the field or looked upon as child-like adults incapable of handling responsibilities. With this background, it is no coincidence that we see the high rates of social issues regarding African-Americans; however, it appears that a great number of people disregard the legacy which bred that ugly machine. And isn't it convenient for those lovers of the Euro-American history to leave this and other ugly chapters out of the history lessons of the development of this nation. Until a decade ago you could hardly bring to justice a person who committed a hate crime against a person, particularly if that person's color was black.

Now in our present era, the powers that be have decided to allow the current process of racial profiling to continue, remember lynching in America. Again, they have made the decision to play god-like in their selection of the elimination of a population group that they deem as expendable. However, progressive and spiritual-minded American citizens must work together to head off the political and social injustice currently developing into the 21ˢᵗ Century Plantation. It's a very sick world when men who wear badges harass and destroy the lives of some blacks instead of protecting them. The current system robs many blacks of their economic mobility by incarcerating their young men while another segment receives more humane and sometimes preferential treatment for the same type of offenses. Have we again turned a blind eye to the problem of race in America? Do we believe it's still the 80s and race issues and concerns will just go away? Police misconduct and abuse is still rampant. Maybe it is a low-level error in judgement as far as interviews and job placement, or could it be that these gatekeepers or overseers represent the policy of the emerging second post-reconstruction era in America, a policy of neglect and incarceration. Hitler got his basic model for Nazism from the Early American model of slavery. Some race supremacists disguised as police, politicians, corporate heads, or one who has succumbed to this form of hate can be seen as an organized system that has bred much of our fear of prejudice and of our dramatic social unrest issues. However, those who turn a deaf ear to the problem whatever their race, religion or occupation, are guilty as the supremacist. For example, we have worked together as citizens in order to prevent criminal governmental behavior such as in Waco. Therefore, we must prevent the conspiracy to restore a plantation system entering into the 21ˢᵗ Century as well.

Criminals should not have the opportunity to lock up non-criminals, such as the SS in Germany and the Southern police forces during the Civil Rights struggle in America. When those who wear badges have the feeling of absolute power and protection, the result may send home to our youth the message that the governmental system is basically criminal. Then what we may get for the future of American society are militia groups, gangs, and an overall breakdown of our socioeconomic infrastructure. This breakdown might occur, because Americans would have lost faith in the American government to protect its people as guaranteed in our Constitution.

Roman society did not fall from outside invasion, but it fell from the inside due to social and moral breakdown. Therefore, let us learn from history that social and moral degeneration through our own government and its people will ultimately cause America's fall if we don't prevent the rise of hate in America.

Four hundred years ago slavery was the law. Now it appears that subtle social reaction such as racial profiling and adjudication has created a caste system, which is similar to the American Peculiar Institution.

For those who espouse and believe in religion yet hate those who are different, God will judge us on the basis of our hearts. And God will reward or punish all of mankind and America based on our actions: the law of reciprocity. You can observe that we are heading into a century that will present us with great environmental and human challenges. Those who are evil and will not heed our warning signs such as the Pharaohs and the Caesars in history will perhaps cause America to suffer the same fates. But those who see and act to change what is going on, may help to prevent an American decline.

IV. CONCLUSION

Although this book has been written primarily to focus on a particular group's struggle throughout the last decade of the century regarding prejudice. My addition of this chapter is an attempt to explain the black experience in order to demonstrate prejudice in general by using a specific model. I feel that the chapter is both objective and subjective; however, I believe it to be a relevant document. The Plantation 21st Century chapter should be looked at with a color-blind level of understanding. If the group discussed were women or white males treated in the same fashion, then would the chapter have made the readers feel any differently? I hope not. However, the reality is probably so. The history of America tells us that race differences are a major factor in how people are treated. Even in the African-American experience, the hue of a person sometimes dictates status. "If you're white you're alright, if you're brown hang around, if you're black stay back." It is not quite the fact, but its legacy still lingers in the American psyche.

This document will probably raise all kinds of human emotions. However, my attempt is to raise the American consciousness. For some, the road to elevating consciousness may be difficult; but for others it is a spiritual odyssey that has been occurring for some time now. Nonetheless, many have contributed to the civil rights improvements in America for all. The words of the Constitution are mankind's attempt to express his ideal of an equal and just society for all Americans. However, if we are to lead the world we must lead by example and not by words.

Some people cannot seem to accept or are in denial about the dark side of the development of this country. The dispossessing of the Native-Americans and the enslavement of Africans are examples of moral cancers that have plagued our nation to this day. The emergence of race supremacy and hatred continues to divide our nation despite all of the new changes in civil rights laws and education.

Let us go into the 21st Century united for the cause of survival and to overcome the plagues of our past, and to create a better world for our children and our children's children. Let us stop teaching hate and violence and let us begin teaching charity and brotherhood. Let us begin this century with New Hope and New Vision for our future generations. Those of us who are progressive spiritual thinkers, let us learn to walk in each other's shoes in order to better understand each other. We must learn to see each other as different parts of the "One". This document is intended to be a proactive course of awareness toward the raising of our consciousness to the American Constitution.

Literary and Abstract Surveys of Socioeconomic Issues of Blacks in Pursuit of High Level Education

OUTLINE

Literary and abstract surveys of socioeconomic issues
of blacks in pursuit of a high-level education

I. Introduction

II. Literary Summary—"Black Bourgeoisie"

III. Abstracts and Surveys
A. "Black College Day"
B. Desegregation Plan: Virginia College

C. The Black Colleges: A Strategy of Relevancy
D. The Trickle-Down Effect
E. Demand for Black Studies
F. Bigots in the Ivory Tower

CHAPTER 4

Introduction

*LITERARY SUMMARIES
AND ABSTRACT SURVEYS*

Written over ten years ago, this section of abstracts and surveys were included to assess where American was headed concerning race and prejudice through the observations and words of the author. These literary works help document the prophetic insights into the America race dilemma which we are now facing.

INTRODUCTION

The importance of Section B concerns the writer's use of abstracts and literary surveys to explain the mood, needs, and issues concerning the area of Afro-American education enrichment during this era of Post Integration.

The section on E. Franklin Frazier's work the "Black Bourgeoisie" highlights some of the relationships past and contemporary, affecting the socioeconomic progress in relation to problems of Afro-American achievement, especially in the area of cultural education.

The section concerning the abstract surveys primarily focuses on contemporary problems and issues facing blacks in the pursuit of higher education and economic mobility in general during the period of Post-Integration. This information should help reader to update, comprehend, and see major issues concerning the realities of the state of Black America regarding social and educational development.

CHAPTER 5

Literary Summary
"Black Bourgeoisie"

*LITERARY SURVEY OF TWO HIGHLY RECOMMENDED
READINGS CONCERNING AMERICA'S RACE ISSUES*

LITERARY SUMMARY—"BLACK BOURGEOISIE"

The Black Bourgeoisie is a study and analogy of the emergence of the black middle class in America. It covers the history of the Black American from slavery through Reconstruction to the years immediately proceeding the Civil Rights Era. The book is mainly divided into two sections—Part I, which is entitled The World of Reality and Part II, The World of Make-Believe. Part I explores the roots, education, power, political orientation and economic basis of middle-class status as well as other areas that aided in the formation and birth of the black bourgeoisie. Part II explores the different levels in which the author believes the black middle-class has deluded itself into an artificial system of acceptance without any type of substantive racial pride. The areas covered in this section include the black business, the society status, the part the black press plays in propagating certain myths and what is really underneath this carefully constructed, self-deceptive, fantasy world.

The author of this book, E. Franklin Frazier, was a leading sociologist that was Professor and Chairman of the Department of Sociology at Howard University. During his writing career, he produced other studies of the black experience such as the black family and the black American in the United States. In recognition of this particular literary effort, he received the MacIver Award of the American Sociological Association. Dr. Frazier, who was also president of the American Sociological Association, died in May of 1962.

This study is generally a well-organized and clearly written examination. The chapters are written and arranged in a chronological manner that moves from the most basic stage of understanding and then progresses on to stages which are progressively more complex in structure.

As a historian, Dr. Frazier is definitely from the revisionist school of thought because his historical information understandably includes quite a bit of information that is almost consistently overlooked in the books written by the traditional classical historians. The sources used in this study are mainly secondary but there was also the usage of actual interviews from the middle-class blacks of various ages. There were also quite a bit of historical references including mini-biographies of influential blacks in various eras as well as examples and excerpts taken from a variety of periodicals familiar to the black Americans such as Ebony and Jet, in addition to numerous other publications. This book is therefore, well documented and although quite a bit of the book tends to be in author's opinion, he does manage to support his main theme fairly well with adequate information.

One method that was used frequently was the insertion of numerous statistics on virtually every subject covered in this study. The statistics are compiled from information that is, at best twenty-nine years old and because quite a bit of changes have occurred during that period of time, the book takes on a heavily dated appearance. This proves to be quite a distraction for the reader and it becomes more acute with the passage of time. It appears that the work would have been more effective if it did not contain quite so many numerical facts stated as present statistics that would become obsolete in the foreseeable future. The one advantage that the usage of those statistics presents is that it allows the reader, in the 90's for instance, to see just how many things have changed in the black middle class and society at large.

The material itself is written reasonably well and because of the content I found it to be very thought provoking. There were many things that were familiar as a result they demanded further thought within to determine the personal worth and or validity and acceptance to be given to the work. This had to be done during the reading because although this was a quality study, the author tended to hold the black middle-class as a whole in contempt. Although most of his points were accurate and well founded, there was little praise of the positive aspects of the achievements or intentions of the black middle-class.

Dr. Frazier set out to discuss and prove how the middle-class was excluded from white America and as a result, embarked upon a course that not only did not alter their position in white society but also separated them from the little bit of roots and culture that black Americans had managed to acquire during their brief time in North America. He was successful on most points and because of this, the book would be excellent reading for all, especially progressive-minded black Americans who are sincerely interested in understanding and taking an honest look at themselves and their environment to aid themselves in deciding how they intend on developing and maximizing their real potential.

CHAPTER 6

Abstracts and Surveys

A. "Black College Day"
B. Desecration Plan: Virginia College
C. The Black College:
A. Strategy of Relevancy
D. The Trickle-Down Effect
E. Black Higher Education
F. Demand for Black Studies
G. Bigots in the Ivory Tower

A. "BLACK COLLEGE DAY"

BIBLIOGRAPHICAL REFERENCE:

Brown, Tony, <u>Black College Day</u>, The National Movement to Save Black Colleges, Tony Brown pub. New York, 1982.

DEFINITION OF TERMS:

Desegregation is the idea of abolishing racial segregation.

Black Colleges are institutions that are populated by predominantly black men and women pursuing degrees in professional fields.

Separatism is the idea of dividing, keeping apart, and making distinct barriers due to race, creed and/or religion.

AUTHOR'S PURPOSE:

The author's purpose was to bring attention to a modern day dilemma: integration and desegregation that is harmful to black colleges and black achievement. He states, in this article, that the survival of black colleges and socioeconomic development is in doubt due to integration. Also, he focuses on the recent separate events around our country concerning what blacks are doing to hold onto their institutions such as the suite against the state of Pennsylvania by Cheyney State College, and a rally in Washington, D.C., of black students and civil rights leaders demonstrating for the survival of black colleges.

MAIN IDEAS OR BODY:

There are two main ideas in this article, the first of which is that there is a fight to desegregate the black colleges. The federal and state governments are pursuing desegregation procedures as if the black colleges perpetuated segregation and separatism. The government has forgotten the reason why black colleges existed in the past. The black students were at that time excluded from the mainstream of white society and denied an equal chance to attend the white colleges, therefore, the product of this became the black college.

The other main idea is that the dismantling of black colleges would stifle the (socioeconomic) progress of blacks by keeping blacks from finishing and attaining degrees from mainly accredited four year institution. It is a fact that when you compare the 90 (ninety) black colleges to 1,500 (fifteen hundred) white colleges, both graduate, on average, the same number of blacks. Needless to say, black colleges are serving a vital role in the survival and success of black communities.

CONCLUSIONS:

In conclusion, take black colleges out of the picture and we will lose fifty percent of all blacks that graduate every year from college. Afro-Americans could not afford it, or America.

RECOMMENDATIONS AND IMPLICATIONS FOR EDUCATION:

I recommend this newsletter of this journal to be distributed into the hands of blacks in order for them to use their hands to build our black colleges so that they can survive the challenge from those who are threatening their existence.

B. DESEGREGATION PLAN:
Virginia College

BIBLIOGRAPHICAL REFERENCE:

Bohlen, Celestine, Vexing Virginia College Desegregation Plan Now in Robb's Lap, Washington Post, Monday, 6 September 1982.

AUTHOR'S PURPOSE:

The author's purpose was to bring to light the problems facing Governor Robb. His problems stemmed from his losing some one hundred million dollars from the education budget effective that year unless he complied with the 1978 Civil Rights Act of desegregating Virginia's public colleges.

MAIN IDEAS:

The main points are three-fold, involving a problem that started in Virginia in 1619. Equalizing the education for black students in Virginia and other states, in order to satisfy black leaders and to comply with the Civil Rights Act and to tell the basic fundamental problems facing the state's objective in meeting the needs of black students in order not to have the funds for education cut off.

Virginia public schools and colleges cannot accommodate the needs for black students because of poor planning and backward approaches towards the improvement of education for blacks. Some suggest that by improving the high schools' role in preparing black students for college, it will enable the schools to go through a desegregation plan smoothly, but unless this step is heated up, implementation of any desecration efforts will not help stop the eradicating existing black socioeconomic dilemma.

<u>CONCLUSIONS:</u>

In summation of this article, Virginia and elsewhere has the delicate task of trying to eradicate the vestiges of de facto segregation in higher education. It is also a complex task, involving not only racial attitudes but also education theories and the never-easy relationship between state government and education boards.

<u>RECOMMENDATIONS AND IMPLICATIONS FOR EDUCATION:</u>

I recommend this article for those people, especially black people interested in the education process, especially in higher education in Virginia's schools. This article is informative, straightforward, concise and factual.

C. THE BLACK COLLEGES:
A Strategy for Relevancy

BIBLIOGRAPHICAL REFERENCE:

LeMelle, Tilden & Wilbert J., <u>The Black College—A Strategy for Relevancy</u>, Praeger Pub. Co., New York 1969.

DEFINITION OF TERMS:

The Ideology of Accommodation is the ideology of ineffective adaptability. In the context of conflict, it is an ideology that aims to please the opposition, rather than resolve the conflict.

The Ideology of Reconciliation is a philosophy of compromise. It means is through confrontation of the purpose of resolving a conflict. The ultimate goal of the reconciliation is to abolish racism and the assimilation into the majority of white society. The goals are the same as above but the means are different.

The Ideology of Separation: Black Nationalism is the idea aimed at creating a group-oriented rationale as a new order. It supports physical and geographic separation, puts self interest and pride first and above all else believes that the destiny of the black man is not going to materialize along the ideologies of accommodation and reconciliation.

The Ideology of Black Mobilization is an idea that rejects assimilation into the white majority but is a synthesis of the three ideologies within the black community. They see the other three ideologies operative but put no emphasis on physical association per se. It eschews the geographic separate philosophy of the Nationalist but along with group pride and interest, it encompasses the principle of black self-reliance above all else.

Black Liberal Idealism is an idea that believes in the true ideals and values of American liberal society. Black is used to identify black Americans subscribing to their philosophy rather than to ideology with a peculiar black content. They tend to believe in goodness over evil in the support for freedom.

AUTHOR'S PURPOSE:

The author's reason for writing this chapter was to break through the rhetoric of the behavioral scientists of their preoccupation with methodologies and theory building. They wanted to give a clear and practical behavioral scientific analysis of black colleges and to give answers to problems facing black colleges and blacks in general, instead of leaving the work of solving problems to the social engineers who understand little about the problems and less about scholars' analyses.

MAIN IDEAS OF BODY:

Author's central message focuses on blacks in higher education. The main message breaks down into supporting details concerning the whole picture of blacks in higher education. The supporting details are black ideologies, past theories and goals for the future.

CONCLUSION:

This is an important article to those interested in the understanding of terminology's which social scientist, scholar and enlightened people generally use to explain many of the socioeconomic dynamics of the Black American Dilemma.

RECOMMENDATION:

I recommend this article to students, scholars, and all concerned citizens interested in a review or enlightenment of the Black American Dilemma in social behavioral terms.

D. THE TRICKLE-DOWN EFFECT

<u>BIBLIOGRAPHICAL REFERENCE:</u>
Williams, Dennis, The Trickle-Down Effect, Newsweek, New York, NY, Sept. 20, 1982.

<u>DEFINITION OF TERMS:</u>
Trickle Down Effect is know as rising college costs, the recession and cuts in federal student aid which caused somewhat of a re-emergence of a class society on American campuses.

<u>AUTHOR'S PURPOSE:</u>
The author's purpose was to show what has happened to the students for jmakl classes of American society during this fall's enrollment in American College campuses, private and public, due to the trickle down effect.

<u>MAIN IDEAS OR BODY:</u>
The main idea is America's black and poor student are prevented from attending large universities and private colleges due to the high cost of tuition and the fear of no financial aid, and its systematic process of declining black and low income student enrollment in general from the past. The combination of the two works as an effective means of educational inequality by pricing blacks and low income people out of the education market.

<u>CONCLUSIONS:</u>
The systematic process of eliminating the chance for blacks to attend any college of their choice despite financial background has reappeared again in the form of a disguise of recession, but actually it is nothing more than the old class war of the past between the haves and the have nots.

RECOMMENDATIONS AND IMPLICATIONS FOR EDUCATION:

These two implications are important concerning all Americans:

I. The loss of black and lower income students from large universities and private colleges will have adverse effects on American society and will again cause tremendous problems in the social and economic areas of the nation on top of the current recession woes.

II. Already some of the social scientists are talking about the reduction of black undergraduates due to forced desegregation of America's black colleges. The fact is clear that education for blacks is the target area to stifle black Americans' progress in gaining their 'piece of the pie' in America.

E. BLACK HIGHER EDUCATION

BIBLIOGRAPHICAL REFERENCE:

Loam, Louis E., Black Higher Education, The Negro Revolt—Pain and Progress, New York, NY, Sept. 20, 1982.

MAIN THEME:

In America's past, the African slaves were not given the opportunities for education, and this destroyed culture and many other aspects of the Afro-American. The reasons for these atrocious acts were that blacks were intellectually inferior and therefore uneducable and that by keeping blacks away from an education, they would remain inferior to whites.

Blacks however, did learn despite many negative factors. Blacks became thinkers and leaders in their respected communities and from these communities grew five basic ideologies, which now constitutes the various ideas of black survival in America. Each clearly outline a constructive, non-violent plan in order to get their fair share of the piece of the pie in America. The goal, therefore, was a strong educational system that would include a national plan which would be the identification of cultural ties to the mother land, Africa, the legitimization of aspirations of American blacks, and to develop attitudes conducive to group politics and meaningful participation in the race of a competitive economy.

CONCLUSIONS:

In summarization, this chapter states that if the black education can be attentive to the socializing aspects and just as attentive in its function for preparing students to man jobs, it will fulfill its role in the black community. The Black-American will be fortified with what he needs for getting his 'piece of the pie' in U.S. society and the ambivalence concerning the attitudes of the white majority race about the role of black higher education will be eliminated for centuries to come.

<u>RECOMMENDATIONS AND IMPLICATIONS FOR EDUCATION:</u>

The writer recommends that this book become a part of all Black-Americans' libraries. It should be a road map for black leaders, educators, churches and civic organizations in addressing the goals, history and status of Black-Americans. Great reading: factual, concise and good to all sixteen and over.

F. DEMAND FOR BLACK STUDIES

BIBLIOGRAPHICAL REFERENCE:

Hebning, Robert, <u>Demand for Black Studies</u>, The Final Call Pub. Chicago, Sept. 16, 1988

AUTHOR'S PURPOSE:

The author's purpose of the article is to bring into light the current imbalance of the curriculum taught to black youth during this era of post-integration in America, in order to help counter the socioeconomic decline of Afro-Americans.

MAIN IDEA:

It is through history that a culture learns the values, concepts, principles and theories which are the foundational aspects of Self-Identity, Political and Socioeconomic Philosophical Development; however, for the masses of black Americans, the curriculum of history has often reflected the majority culture in America. Therefore, Afro-Americans has been the victims of institutional cultural and historical ignorance making the socioeconomic achievements of Afro-Americans foundationally inferior.

CONCLUSION:

Afro-Americans is deprived of a balance curriculum in contrast of rising standards on basic subjects; during post-integration's, America has not opted to improve the balance given the psycho/social importance.

G. BIGOTS IN THE IVORY TOWER

BIBLIOGRAPHICAL REFERENCE:

Tifft, Susan, <u>Bigots in the Ivory Tower</u>, Time Magazine, January 23, 1989.

AUTHOR'S PURPOSE:

The purpose of this article was to bring to light in a major literary publication the recent mood on college campuses during this era of post-integration in America, the comeback of racial, sexual, and religious prejudice.

MAIN IDEAS:

This generation of intolerance is observed through the (mico-cosm microcosm) of the national political climate and the ignorance of the past struggles regarding racial and general civil right issues.

The growing trend of bigotry will return to America's college campuses as long as students remain complacent in their insensitivity and ignorance and feel that the national mood of American society, especially white America is in support of this trend.

CONCLUSION:

America's College Campuses are basically the testing thermostats of the National trend that the youth feel are society's feelings.

RECOMMENDATIONS AND IMPLICATIONS FOR EDUCATION:

I recommend this article to all concerned over the issues of race problems in America society.

CHAPTER 7

CLEAR WARNINGS . . . RACISM STILL EXISTS TODAY

EXAMPLE OF A SOLUTION BELL/MEAC - A MODEL OF SUCCESS

CLEAR WARNINGS
RACISM STILL EXISTS TODAY

Although America has come a long way since the time of the Middle Passage through the days of segregation, it is evident that hatred still thrives and continues to this day. Neo-Nazi's, The Arian Brotherhood and the Klan are enjoying a significant resurgence. The Rev. Richard Butler and William Pierce, authors of the Turner Diaries—a blueprint for present and future ethnic cleansing, have spread their hatred and beliefs to a new generation of supporters. New White Power fanatics continue to spread their lies and myths of race superiority and the impurity of America. Descendants of Fritz Kuhn, Adolph Hitler and Norman Rockwell continue to perpetuate a pseudo-scientific and religious dogma through the decades. It is amazing that history's most significant villain, Adolph Hitler is still idolized and his teachings followed still today.

Our society is seemingly producing an alarming rate of youths with an overwhelming need for peer acceptance and attention. Although adolescence and life in general can be overwhelming at times, this group is being led by their insecurities. They are often searching for understanding and love, but instead find the message of violence and hatred. Gang violence and racial hatred are at an all time high. We must stop and readjust our attitudes. We must create systems to channel these insecurities into positive actions and multi-cultural beliefs.

In our fast-paced society, we Americans seldom pay close attention to the important and dangerous underlining issues. Issues that at the time seem not to affect us personally, however, the problems regarding race and hatred affect us all. Therefore prejudice will not end until all Americans learn to understand and accept our differences. It is time to dispel the myths of racial superiority and inferiority. It is time to accept our differences in skin color, religion and heritage. Groups that idolize hate mongers of the past should be exposed and taken seriously. Acts of racial violence and hatred must no longer be accepted. Americans must watch the warning signs of the past, find peaceful resolutions to our problems, and educate our new generation to understand and embrace our differences.

BELL/MEAC
A Model of Success

In order to affect a change in the future, we must first uncover and understand the past. Earlier chapters have described the struggles the first African-Americans faced in slavery, the foundation of racial superiority and inferiority and the names and teachings of racists through our history.

You can now understand the devastating effects of prejudice, racism and hatred. It's time to write a new chapter in American History and change our attitudes and perceptions. It is time to devise a positive plan of action.

THE BELL/METROPOLITAN EDUCATIONAL ACHIEVEMENT CLUB

INTRODUCTION

Recently, scholars have begun to focus attention on the causes and effects of racial problems in our society, and particularly on youth and violence. These issues are no longer a direct reaction to socio-economic conditions, but rather cross all socio-economic barriers.

Mr. Phillip Bell, Jr., MA, author of Run In My Shoes, and A Social Study of the Causes and Effects of Racial Problems in Black History and a Plan for the Re-education of Today's Black Youth, has not only studied the causes and effects but has enacted a plan-of-action to challenge what has become the status quo.

Mr. Bell's study, completed in 1989, is still relevant today. He presents the origins of racial problems from the 17th Century to the present in America, effects of socio-economic issues of Blacks and education, and presents strategies for addressing the long-term future for Black youth in America.

His plan is a proven one, as demonstrated by his Metropolitan Educational Achievement Club (MEAC) operating in the Metropolitan Washington, D.C. area since 1987. MEAC is a recreational therapy program for at-risk youth and their families providing a wide variety of services ranging from swimming, horseback riding and team sports to academic tutoring, counseling, stress management and conflict resolution training.

The Metropolitan Educational Achievement Club has gained the attention and praise from area school administrators, the Washington, D.C. Department of Human Services, the Washington, D.C. Juvenile Court System, the Alexandria, Virginia Department of Mental Health, Mental

Retardation and Substance Abuse, Alexandria, Virginia Schools and Social Services, and more.

Phillip Bell understands the problems that face today's at-risk youth and continues to offer viable solutions. He has developed a feasible plan to turn the disturbing trend of youth-violence and racial inequities around with his sound, proven ability to reach, teach and understand.

In order to share the ongoing success of his MEAC program, Phillip Bell has developed several plans of action and is available to:

(5) Speak at group functions for youth and families.

(6) Provide consultation services, for start-up services, using his successful MEAC program as the model.

(7) Provide expert views during panel discussions of these and related issues.

Our children are our future, don't allow societies pre-set conditions to continue. Together we can help today's youth begin to gain a greater awareness and appreciation for life. Let Phillip Bell's success become your own, call him today for an overview and initial consultation. 301.283.6858.

The primary goal of the MEAC program is to provide a positive atmosphere and planned services for building self-esteem, self-identity, cultural awareness, character, overall metal and physical fitness and health. The Metropolitan Education Achievement Club (MEAC) is a non-profit educational organization in the Washington, DC area founded to improve the achievement of black students and to:

1. Aid black and all teenagers in becoming successful, productive citizens through culturally sensitive, yet down-to-earth support systems.

2. Aid specialized agencies such as schools, churches and shelters. In addition, unlike most organizations, Bell/MEAC creates a positive peer environment that stresses optimism and achievement.

STATEMENT OF PROBLEM

Bell/MEAC specializes in providing programs for black youth ages 6 to 16. Many with few economic resources, low self-esteem, identity issues, lack of positive role models, academic stress, and in some instances volatile attitudes. However, we have found these children are far from hopeless. They can and will overcome these obstacles with education, care, motivation and firm direction.

ANALYSIS OF PROBLEM

The teen years are difficult for all; they are a time of personal changes and emotional upheavals. Teens often drop out of school or get into trouble mainly due to their inability to cope with their changes in body image, identity, and environment. The teen years are a high-risk period. This risk is markedly increased for black youths. In many instances their homes are frequently single-parented with few economic resources. Their communities too often lack positive role models, and peer-pressure to act in potentially dangerous or criminal ways is constantly threatening.

The schools, churches, and recreational settings offer some acceptable social outlets and cultural enrichment, however the average school system still reflects the majority culture of America. Often times, the system does not provide the full cultural and social support often needed during the crucial teen years. Schools have also been unsuccessful in significantly raising the academic level of our black youth. A solution to reduce the risks associated with adolescence and the state of being a black teenager must be developed and supported or an entire generation may be threatened by drug addiction, unwanted pregnancies, volatile attitudes and illiteracy unseen in modern times. Bell/MEAC provides the social, emotional, and cultural support that may be lacking in these youths' environment.

STATEMENT OF NEED

It is not a coincidence that over seven-hundred thousand students per year since 1985 are dropping out of high school, and many more graduate illiterate, not even having the basic skills to read a magazine or comprehending simple instructions for household appliances. Too many students leave without having learned discipline, or the responsibility for assigned tasks. Many adolescents do not choose the merits of education, because economically a life of crime may prove more advantageous and profitable.

In public schools nationwide, a new agenda concerning minority achievement is currently popular. Many programs are designed to help students in the classrooms and on test taking skills; however, Bell/MEAC has a focus on developing the consciousness and sub-consciousness in order to help adolescents feel more positive about themselves and their community.

Bell/MEAC continues in its efforts because teens continue to grow in an era where they are facing newer conflicts and challenges in America's attempt to deal with parity of education and race relations. Bell/MEAC's focus centers directly with the socialization process within the schools. The goal being to help black students become psychologically capable of becoming functional in schools, homes and communities.

PURPOSE OF PROJECT

Bell/MEAC seeks to help the black teen adjust psychologically during this phase of American evolutionary process of integration; for the purposes of this project, psychological adjustment means the black teen will have more concern for fellow students' social accountability. They will develop an awareness of their present state of functioning; they will have a better focus on why they are here; where and how they fit into society presently and in the future. Basically, they will have developed an improved sense of social accountability. It is expected that they will have enhanced self-pride, a positive self-image, a greater self-motivation, and greater self-control. Finally, Bell/MEAC seeks to provide encouragement to uncover the rich Afro-American historical influence and focus on current trends and issues concerning the development and growth during the difficult teens years.

PROGRAM OBJECTIVES

1. To provide a framework of understanding of culture and history of Afro-Americans, and the roles each played in the development and achievement in America.

2. To strengthen the academic performance by enhancing students' understanding of what a role model is and to translate the sense of self-worth and accomplishment into strategies on how to develop and set goals for personal achievement.
3. To provide emotional support.
4. To provide an environment of positive peer pressure.
5. To encourage well-rounded citizenship, such as concern for self and others; and
6. To enhance physical fitness, sportsmanship, and teamwork.

PROJECT METHODOLOGY

POSITIVE PEER PRESSURE CLUBS/GROUPS: Positive peer pressure clubs is the catalyst for planning Bell/MEAC. The strategy is to attract students back into an academic mind-set by developing a positive peer pressure group that gives its members motivation and reinforcement. The behavioral modification system will reward its members, thereby, reinforcing academic and social progress.

The way it works is to establish a core group of interested and motivated students, who will have a mission to uphold Bell/MEAC ideals while helping to recruit other students who have the interest and potential to follow suit. From these established leaders, the goal is to cause a "domino effect" of positive peer pressure within the particular school or community where Bell/MEAC is serving.

An important aspect of the program is to reinforce the philosophy of "Learn and Earn" legally, thus a contract-reward schedule is set in place. Also, files will be developed on club members that include contracts of activities designed to shape a well-rounded adolescent in society. Fulfillment of contracts will result in rewards and special activities.

COUNSELING: Bell/MEAC places an emphasis on Humanistic Social/ Behavioral Therapy. The importance of successfully developing Bell/ MEAC will begin with peer counselors who will be responsible for handling the following psychological and human developmental issues regarding: (1) Health, (2) Crisis Intervention (3) Afro-American, (4) Adolescent Psychological Issues, and (5) Motivational Counseling.

Bell/MEAC is of the opinion that intimate sharing of feelings, ideas, experiences in an atmosphere of mutual respect and understanding enhances self-respect, deepens self-understanding and helps a person live with others.

POSITIVE ROLE-MODELS: In the areas of enhancing the perception of positive role models club members, ten to twenty black speakers from the community will be invited to share their life experiences, expertise, or just information concerning issues and trends confronting teens. This array of information will shape the consciousness and sub-consciousness perception of whom to emulate in society and to go to for direction and information during those very challenging per-adult years.

PHYSICAL FITNESS: Another important goal is to reinforce to black teens to place emphasis on the minimums one can take to achieve good physical health. The major focus will be on developing a schedule for exercise in order to improve the cardiovascular system and overall appearance. The basic activities center on group and individual activities that involve physical exertion conductive to the interests and environment at which the club is located. We also provide written information in order to educate teens of the overall importance of good health.

Bell/MEAC provides creative experiences such as picnics, tours, hikes, retreats, sports and other activities for members and occasionally include other family members as well. Retreats are held during the summer vacation and other prescribed vacation months. this activity designed to stimulate the adolescents' consciousness concerning the natural environment, simple living, the youth love affair with camping, and a change for urban youth that rarely have a chance to live in a natural environment.

PROJECT STAFFING

To implement our programs, BELL/MEAC draws on volunteer services of its original members as well as concerned citizens. For example, teachers, business leaders, community leaders, local artists, and elected officials are just some of the people who partner with BELL/MEAC and counsel students and present programs. To mobilize and organize these volunteers BELL/MEAC also depends on the following personal:

BOARD OF DIRECTORS: The Board acts as advisors, public relations coordinators, and primarily fund-raisers. The BELL/MEAC Board meets bimonthly and consults with one another and staff concerning the overall projections and operations of the program.

CHAIRMAN OF THE BOARD: The Chairman's responsibility is to make final decisions in areas, such as: spending, program development plans, hiring, firing, salary negotiations, and overall directorship of the entire program.

EXECUTIVE DIRECTOR: The Executive Director has the responsibility of supervising and managing Bell/MEAC programs as well as overseeing administrative tasks at the center, and finally to be responsible for all fund disbursements.

In consultation with the Board of Directors, the Executive Director establishes the activity calendar and plans the on-going programs. He also assigns tasks for the Bell/MEAC staff and is responsible for training and supervision.

As necessary, the Executive Director locates volunteer resources through out the community. He works closely with volunteers, supervising their work when appropriate. He schedules regular and volunteer staff and arranges for the implementation of new programs.

PEER COUNSELORS: Peer Counselors are responsible to the authority of the Director and report directly as such. Their overall responsibilities include counseling, monitoring, mentoring and the over-all development of the positive-peer pressure groups for club members.

Peer Counselors also coordinate the activities in the Bell/MEAC in-school clubs. They regularly attend club meetings and work to establish additional clubs in other schools and to promote the Bell/MEAC Program.

ADMINISTRATIVE ASSISTANT (PT): The administrative assistant is responsible for clerical duties to ensure efficiency of the operation. Such duties include, but would not be limited to: typing of correspondence and other center-related documents, maintaining files, and receiving and routing visitors.

PROJECT EVALUATION

(1) (1.) A high indicator for evaluation will be based on Bell/MEAC keeping a numeric roster of the participating club members on a daily, weekly, monthly and yearly basis.

(2) (2.) The opinions of club members from time to time will be sought regarding strengths, weaknesses, and suggestions for evaluation.

(3) (3.). A Before-and-After Survey will be administered to parents, members, and staff concerning the overall expectations of BELL/MEAC services and activities, particularly as they relate to the promotion of self-awareness, pride, and social accountability.

TIME TABLE

In addition to BELL/MEAC's day-to-day activities, many services are rendered which are seasonal in nature. The following timetable is a calendar of projected events during the calendar year:

First Quarter—January - March:

BELL/MEAC supports its talents and energies towards helping in the commemoration of Black History and begins developing a list of talented role models for the third quarter symposiums and seminars.

Second Quarter—April - June:

BELL/MEAC develops seminars and symposiums for community efforts and programs. A wide variety of people, such as historians, political members, actors, musicians, and other positive role models are featured during this quarter.

Third Quarter—July - September:

BELL/MEAC organizes a series of weekly and weekend retreats as well as day-today outings to special recreational areas. Also, BELL/MEAC has bimonthly picnics at area parks for members and their families.

Fourth Quarter—October - December:

BELL/MEAC places focus on educational and cultural field trips to historic, enlightening, and entertaining places in the Washington, DC area.

Teaching new skills to Bell/MEAC Students

Bell/MEAC Student

Bell/MEAC Students

Bell/MEAC Counselor and Students

Phillip with Bell/MEAC Students

**Chuck (left). Nubia (center). Ivory (right).
Horses used in Equestrian Therapy at Bell/MEAC Ranch**

**PRESENT UPDATE ADDENDUM
(CURRENT UPDATES SINCE THE PRESIDENTIAL
ELECTIONS OF BARACK OBAMA AND DONALD TRUMP
REGARDING AMERICAN RACE RELATIONS.)**

CHAPTER 8

HISTORICAL FACTS ABOUT AFRICA

Historical Facts about Africa, the cradle of Civilization and the rise of the Triangular Slave Trade

Africa is the second largest continent in the world, and the word comes from the Greek word aphrike- meaning without cold or aprica for sunny.

Africa is the birth place of Humans. In 1959 Louis and Mary Leaky made a discovery of remains of human skulls and stone tools that were nearly 2 million years old.

Over a periods of millions of years, some early people left Africa and crossed into Asia. From there descendants or offspring fanned out to populate the planet.

The Old Stone Age lasted from about 500,000 to 10,000 years ago. They shaped knives, axes, and spear points out of stone and even bones. They also lived as hunters and food gatherers moving from place to places pursuing herds across the African plains.

The New Stone Age was the origin of farming between 10,000 BC to 3,500 BC. This process started in Africa and moved into Asia and the Americas. This was the revolution of the cultivation of seeds, wild plants roots. The humans at this time also learned to domesticate some animals for human interests.

Some of the earliest farming villages took place along the Nile river about 5,000 BC. The Nile provided rich soil as a result of it overflowing its banks each year. This provided a food supply; therefore, enabling humans to settle longer in one place, and it allowed humans to devote time to other interests and issues that threatened their survival.

Some of the new interests which developed during 5,000 BC were the construction of pyramids, cities, religion, philosophy, writing, mathematics, sciences, astrology, astronomy, and embalming.

Egypt became the center for cultural exchange, trade, and commerce for humans from other continents such as Greece, Asia, Europe, the Middle East and Rome according to ancient antiquity accounts. Egypt's population was to become the myriad of diffusion into segments of many people of other continents. Egypt's history had been divided into three main periods. The Old Kingdom 2700 BC to 2200 BC, this period was highlighted by the Pharaohs development of writing, science, math and pyramids. The Middle Kingdom 2050 BC to 1800 BC was highlighted by the expansion south into Asia, and the Invasion by the Hyksos, whom had chariots and weapons made of Iron. The New Kingdom period was from 1570 BC to 1090 BC. During this period, Egypt had obtained its heights of power, peace and trade, a one God religious belief, Akhenaton, and woman rulers developed as well. Finally after 1090 BC, Egypt's empire had weakened from Nubians, Asians, Greek, and Roman invaders. Although Egypt was established throughout the beginning of the human evolution revolution, Africa had also given birth to other organized African nations. Nubia, the kingdom of Kush was established about 1000 BC. Also south of Kush, the kingdom of Axum developed around 400 BC. This area today is better known as Ethiopia. Both of these two nations were involved in trade and commerce with other continents along the Mediterranean Sea.

During the periods of AD 500 to about 1600, Africa's western nations began to develop at a high level of trade networks with merchants in the Middle East and North Africa, as well as on a limited basis with some Europeans around 1,500 AD. The main three great western kingdoms often recognized were Ghana, Mali and Songhai.

It is important to note that during Africa's development, many changes would occur as a result of changes in leadership due to outside stronger military expansions. These changes would bring changes in culture, land, resources, and religion. Christianity, a religion based on the teachings of Jesus Christ, a Judean would flourish in the Mediterranean areas and parts of Europe. Axum, modern Ethiopia, became the first African nation to convert over to Christianity. When the religion of Islam swept through parts of northern Africa, Axum refused to follow the wave of change, therefore, giving a rise of division amongst its neighbors.

The religion of Islam became the dominant religion of Ghana, Songhai, and Mali. However, the big problem that halted the great trade from Gold mining and wealth in the West was not Islam, but it would be the failure of the African nations in the west, and in general to speak a universal language. This barrier caused more complicated problems concerning trade and commerce. It was at this time that Ghana engaged in selling other humans from whom they captured during wars with their neighbors. However, these captives were not treated as sub humans. They could often buy or work for their freedom after a period of time. During this period, Ghana would also loose the control of the spread of Islam.

Unlike Ghana, Mali had become a key Muslim nation. However the greatness ended with the death of its king Mansa Musa when he was invaded and also internal conflicts occurred. In Songhai, the trade networks had reached into Asia and Europe. Songhai had conquered regions of Mali. One of their greatest rulers was Sunni Ali 1464 AD -1492 AD. Sunni was a believer in Islam; however, there was a divide in Songhai. The divide took shape in countering many of the particular cultural methods of its practices; therefore, causing a religious issue with other Orthodox North African Islamic believers. After Sunni Ali's death, a more Orthodox leader assumed leadership. After his death, most of the military conquests, social, cultural, and economic reforms were not maintained. In 1591, an army of invaders from Morocco marched in to West Africa with 4,000 men armed with primitive guns. This invasion forever changed Songhai, and apparently the world as it was to an even more violent world we know of today.

Apparently the gun began mankind's accession (Domino Effect) towards the decline of human and life security. It has led to the increase in distress, poverty, madness and overall violence in our modern times. It is to be noted that the doors were swung wide open at this time for European trading in Africa. Columbus at this time would make his voyage to the Americas, giving rise to the Caribbean and Americas slave trade out of Africa.

CHAPTER 9

POST OBAMA

My job as a writer is to always try to maintain objective principles in a very subjective and partisan world as I tackle any lecture and, or writing task on Race. My role is to show folks whom will read my materials or attend my lecture series that I am not a partisan for one side in any given subject. Therefore, my conclusions specifically will come from the outcry of those whom are hurt or sometimes looking at those whom benefit from the actions and, or decisions made by the President and decision makers from one administration to the other.

As an African-American, some may conclude that I swing to the Democratic party and Anti-Trump. However, I am an Independent for the record. My earlier statements that I work at being as fair and objective as my human skills can produce as an educator, and writer, will be my goal regarding explaining the effects of President Trump's political influence, cabinet choices, policies, and socio-economic programs that do effect race relations in America and abroad. Although, some readers whom will judge my document will hold onto views primarily based on ideology, and partisan analogies. Therefore, I know that my task is impossible. However, I am attempting to provide my accounts hopefully to a segment of the population that can look at my conclusions objectively, which is all that I seek. That we can all basically understand the essence of the views without being ideologically negative and hostile to what others may perceive differently. Basically, I hope readers can agree to disagree in order to maintain what makes us so uniquely Americans, "The Freedom of Free Speech"; however, focusing on the facts not opinions.

I will not attempt to write a thesis on all of President Trumps political moves, but to highlight one pro and con moves that will be examined closely by many whom are concerned about Race Issues in America. The

Jeff Sessions appointment to the writer was the greatest profound Racist development that President Trump has made during his Presidency. Anyone whom has followed this politician's career, knows that he has had a history of being on the wrong side of history when it has come to Race Relations in America. However, I am not here to analyze all of his past statements and racial views, but simply looking into two issues from both a pro and con racist affect.

The War on drugs in America has help to enslave and destroy the African-American community socio-economically. Attorney General Sessions recent edict to restore harsh maximum sentences for drug crimes thus reversing the trend by both parties reducing prison time for non-violent drug offenses as well as not using the Private Prisons industry by the Federal government. Therefore, turning the clock backwards towards the mass incarceration trends of people of color.

The horrific treatment customary of private prisons corporations, and the mass incarceration practices by the US government, which has specifically affected disproportionately the socio-economic development of African-Americans and people of color. How can one take seriously, the President when he stated that he would be a President for all the people and his promise to help the Afro-American community better than the Democratic party. This claim of doing better than the democrats while hiring Jeff Sessions and allowing him to reverse a trend towards the mass enslavement of people can be seen as highly insensitive and out of touch with the reality of this political maneuver. As a historian and teacher, I know that at least four phases of white supremacy acts have help to destroy the lives of the African-American community. (1.) The Institution of Slavery; (2.) The Willie Lynch Syndrome; (3.) Jim Crow Laws; and (4.) Co-Intel-Pro/ Mass Incarceration.

President Trump went out and hired a man whom had the pedigree to reverse all of the work that went in to making the bi-partisan changes made in the last eight (8) years to at least improve the injustices and double standards throughout the American criminal justice system. Now America is saddled again to unleash the demonic forces of mass incarceration, which is legal slavery, and the furtherance of our society ever treating the symptoms of poverty and crime while allowing corporations like GRE to fill their prisons for profit primarily and disproportionately with low level non-violent members of the African-American community again. The statistics were so over whelming regarding all of these issues that how could a President Trump make such a selection and then allow Attorney General, Jeff Sessions to turn back the hands of time again. The outcry is apparent, and as a writer on Race relations, I felt it my job to make this point clear to my readers that American leaders and it's citizenry should hold President Trump and Jeff Session accountable for all negative issues that will develop.

My pro action by the President comes not so much regarding his approach and actions but from his political instincts and pragmatism to call out the influx of people settling and coming in illegally to the United States. This issue in my research was what elevated President Trump to win the nomination of the Republican party. Many people on both sides of the aisles and Independents feel that the illegal settlements and entry was simply hurting many poorer whites, and African-American workers by taking the jobs that these groups once held. Agree with him on this or not, this political stance appears to be his most bi-partisan agreement that many American agree needs to be solved. President Trumps legacy on Race relations will be looked at as genius or most likely racist and ethnic phobic.

In conclusion, I am not going to go into all of the numerous issues like Climate Change, Russia, and even more issues concerning Race Relations. I just wanted my readers to look at what areas that this President will be judged on historically concerning Race Relations.

In America, regarding my chronological historical sequence and updated materials on Race Relations In America, regarding my book, "Run In My Shoes", Post Obama, Trump eras of historical political, and personal legacies on America's since the first and second editions of Run In My Shoes were developed.

CHAPTER 10

UPDATE BY AUTHOR

The American Social Climate since the Presidency of Obama regarding Race Relations

Since my almost six decades of life all living in America, I have concentrated on the subject of race for almost four and a half decades. Therefore, I do hope that you not only take into account my life's passion, but perhaps to the degree in which I have consistently pursued an education that would direct my passion towards the truth regarding a subject that continues to be passed on, generation to generation without coming to a solution of how to agree without disagreeing on the pain and legacy of American Racism. Here are just a few views which highlights what many Americans just do not understand, comprehend sociologically, nor feel because, we mostly tend to be a people that generally do not care to feel other's pain. What Run In My Shoes wants the readers to see is what it's like to walk in an African-American person's shoes. Therefore, attempting to comprehend it's past and present realities living under Racism.

The "KKK and white supremacists have always been involved in law enforcement since the beginnings".

"One of the very first police existence was the slave patrols used to catch runaway slaves or to keep slaves in order."

"During the Civil Rights Movement, one of the KKK's first order was to infiltrate police departments, because "the laws don't apply to them if they are the law."

"In 1991, a Neo-Nazi, white supremacist gang were made up of sheriff deputies terrorizing the streets of Lynwood in Los Angeles county."

"Two Florida police officers were fired for being in the KKK in 2014."

A "Louisiana cop fired for being a KKK Neo-Nazi in 2015."

"June 20, 2016, "Texas Officers Fired for Memberships in the KKK."

The above information came from website Racism in America Retrieved July 19 2016

These statistics should be a current stark reminder of the ominous reality concerning the ever developing growth of Racism in America in regards to present day law abiding Afro-Americans can face; the level of PTSD and paranoia effects many black citizens; however, why still do scores of White Americans and law enforcement personnel continue to pass off Racism as an isolated issue, which has very little to do with how a person is treated solely based on the color of a person's skin. The usage of intimidating and dangerous behavior by police seen on video cameras highlight the trauma which continues to haunt America until it can honestly account for Racism like it does account for when America feels threatened by its enemies, such as ISIS or Terrorism.

Since the Presidency of Obama, the most important issues to note during his terms were not concerning his medical health care bill, or his attempt to wind down Bush's aggression in the Middle East, his continuance to double down on Bush's tactics regarding NSA surveillance, his aggression of going after government whistle blowers, but it appears to have been on how much racially divided America is now. Since his term, it's become apparent on how socially different America has become. However, for the sake of my study, I only focused on a small capsule of news regarding his presence as President and the issues regarding Race Relations.

The resurgence of Racism since President Obama's terms as President, has truly given rise to the attention of how people view the American racial divide. This obviously implies that we live in a society that had placed Obama simply under a greater level of scrutiny simply because of the color of his skin. "Every action committed by President Obama was placed under a microscope," Since the former President and his family lived in the White House, it appears that race has become a greater issue that Americans can no longer deny for whatever the reasons. In July 2016, An AP poll revealed that 69% of American felt that race relations have declined in America.

Since 2008, 51% up from 48% of Americans, before the election of President Obama, expressed anti-black attitudes. Now that so many tensions are stemming from brutal and unnecessary killing of blacks by police followed by those police mostly going unpunished even when videos show the actual murders. It appeared that a Black president had very little positive effect when you read the heinous KKK and Neo-Nazi statistical realities in policing; therefore, many may comprehend that these executions without any accountability and responsibility by police, as being a subtle message to blacks and a Black presidency that squashes forever, the notion of change that any efforts for people of color to repeat President Obama's steps in American governmental leadership as president will result in white backlash. The million dollar questions is, Where is America headed after Obama?

Clear Warnings update 2016/2017, where is America headed after President Obama's Presidency?

In order to make America work better, all its citizens should learn about all of the mistakes that were made by all people whom existed before them"

Study the past (history) for one basic purpose:

To learn about the mistakes that were made in the past, so as to be better prepared not to make the same mistakes in the future.

As long as you exist, refer to yourself as a permanent student. Without studying the knowledge of our history, we are likely to repeat the same ills into the present and future. At present, it appears since the first and second editions of Run In My Shoes, my pro-active attempt to stimulate discussions towards healthier race relations had somewhat stalled. Then came President Obama, and now President Trump. I tried then, and I am presently attempting to help educate citizens with an update concerning the issues of American Racism. Until the election of the first person of color, President Obama, we have witnessed nothing less than a fire storm of controversies, injustices, racial tensions and division unlike any time since the 60's. Therefore, what I had succinctly intended to create was a series of community town hall forums that would promote team building activities, and dialogs concerning Race relations in America.

At present, it seems that America is currently witnessing a similar historical cycle, like during the 60's Civil Rights Movement. America was then a hotbed at the time of racial division similar to what we are seeing during President Obama's term. Now there are a number of GOP conservatives whom are using a newer version of the 1968 presidential election strategy termed the Southern Strategy which was implemented by Richard Nixon in order to cause fear and to assign the victimization of Afro-Americans to African-Americans instead of to the corrupt or mentally ill police and grand jury system. Several Afro-American Protest groups are categorized as Anarchist for using their second amendment rights to protest against police misconduct. Similarly, Dr. Martin Luther King, Jr., and other civil right leaders were categorized as communist anarchist making trouble for the good colored people. Dr. King at the time was the FBI's most dangerous man in America portrayed by its leader, J. Edgar Hoover. When will Americans as a whole learn that many of these presidential candidates are feeding into tribal levels of prejudices and fears of those whom they can manipulate into supporting an agenda of some greater oligarchical elite group which just benefits from the divide and conquer game that has been played for centuries. Just like the American Civil War, WWI, WWII, Vietnam, and Iraq, Americans have surrendered its life treasures and its wealth to those whom benefit from the manipulation of false flag events causing the divisions in the variety of people in America and on this planet. These elite societies would like to destroy any unity of the people. These groups just want to control all aspects of resources and garner the wealth for themselves and their cronies. Therefore, I offer my advice to readers in spending more time in reviewing history chapters from Run In My Shoes in order to help sharpen your skills and wisdom of what is here and yet to come if we don't get past the mass propaganda campaigns which divide us. We have great concerns such as, Radiation Poisoning, Climate Change, and the Chemtrail spraying which is affecting us all regardless of race, gender and religion.

I must reiterate this again, please learn history in general. So many Americans do not know recent history as well as the past history of the settling by Europeans of the Americas, the up-rooting of the Native Americans, the Peculiar Institution, the Spanish-American Conflict, the Alamo, the Civil Rights Movement, the Civil War and Revolutionary War. Without this small amount of knowledge of American History, it would seem quite difficult to relate to being an American and where it has been, and where it potentially its going. "If you don't know where you've been, then how do you know where you are going."

CHAPTER 11

URGENT PREDICTIONS REGARDING RACE RELATIONS IN AMERICA BY PROFESSOR PHILLIP BELL

Race relations in America after Barrack Obama and Donald Trump

As for the readers of Run in My Shoes, you must know by now, that I have attempted to highlight prejudice and racism in America in order to expose the destructive mental health, economic, and harmful sociological issues which have continued to impact the health and equal prosperity for all Americans. These new updates is my present attempt to bring facts and warnings to my readers regarding the negative social conflicts arising from the major contrasts of President Obama and President Trump's influence on American history. Never in my lifetime have I witnessed such a sense of a possible New Century American Civil War Conflict.

Racism is an historical man-made disease affecting the economic status of America generally affecting people of color by those whom have exploitive powers over them. It has had the greatest impact on Blacks and Native American since the arrival of Europeans to America. Some historians and sociologists blame the victims of the curse of Racism, as if it is a DNA inherited issue regarding why descendants of American Slavery system seem to have so many socio-economic challenges. However, if one honestly examines the races in which groups do have the greatest socio-economic issues, basically, its apparent that racial groups whom were controlled, conquered and systematically culturally destroyed from there natural lives have the most difficulties. Therefore, a careful and fair analysis of the historical legacy of Racism does have an impact on what is obvious in regards to the many socio-economic issues that plague and effect these two major groups of people unless the historical paradigm is examined along with the present analysis can help the present and future generations move past this tribal economic structure. If we fail in the 21st century to do this, we most likely will never have the inner bonding necessary to wipe out this Cancer from America.

Therefore, if people of color, especially Blacks whom are descendants from the 1600's, are going to change their social, political, and economic conditions, they must face the harsh reality that Blacks primarily must take on the full responsibilities for shaping the sociological and economic destiny despite the benign neglect that is apparent in today's society. This will mean looking in the mirror and honestly addressing how splintered and dysfunctional we were molded and developed to not function normally. Blacks whom are descendants of Slavery for at least a couple of centuries have lost community self-help, family structures, safe schools, and control over many of our kids whom do not have all the tools to handle the many obstacles that they do face in a world that has a much more negative perception of Blacks apparently than Blacks have of themselves.

The issues that I am laying out does not attest that all people fall into ascribed categories, however, as a general direction and strategy must develop if Blacks are to re-group their communities and re-shape their ultimate destiny out of the current troubles, and negative factors affecting safety and economic inclusion.

At present the facts are that many of young black males are not keeping up with the ability to compete in the labor force due to the competition of a newer, hungrier, and cheaper labor force. These groups will be used as Africans were used in the South as slaves, to enrich the elite corporations until robots take their spots sometime in the near future. Also, without a stable economic base to hire blacks and to provide self-help, these corporations are only happy to lock blacks away and to use their labor basically the same way that it was used during slavery, while all the time painting the image in the media as they once did during slavery and Jim Crow that blacks are inferior and criminals. Therefore, what we often see in the media is the most negative and dehumanizing images that define black image.

A house divided cannot stand. That is what we are witnessing in America today. Those whom love the country, its people, and have the interest to do the research and work to expose the masterminds of corruption. American need to begin to shut off the entertainment and pursue knowledge and practices from the past to the present which helps to educate the masses about the truth and understanding of why Blacks do suffer from an unique sociological experience. With so many immigrants pouring into America not knowing or understanding the historical genocide socio-economically of blacks, the danger is that these groups will be further brainwashed in believing in the images of blacks.

I have attempted to provide my readers a succinct inquiry and academic study in order to stimulate the long range inquiry of all Americans in facing the truth and realities of Racism and prejudice in which we live in regarding the American legacy. Many folks forget that we truly do live in a spiritual world, as well as a material world. At present, we appear to not think that past, present and future consequences are causes and effects on generally all that the corrupt masterminds orchestrate daily. Wake up America, Blacks descendants are the modern people whom are the Canary in the coal mine.

Native Americans live on reservations dying off from the invasion and conquering of their people. Blacks are facing a similar demise. However, do not think that it cannot happen to you as well. The powers that be have only one true love and image. That image and love is Money, the power that they use to control and manipulate people. Blacks are dealing with an even more sinister plots such as, the Willie Lynch Letter, and the US government Counter Intelligence Program in the 60's. Today it is the Blacktrix, a corporate under class of under educated masses of people whom are divided and conquered by those whom see people only from a Geo-political viewpoint. We are all in the Matrix, but Blacks are in both the Matrix and Blacktrix. This agenda will be an attempt to enslave us all and to systematically depopulate the earth.

CHAPTER 12

RUN IN MY SHOES

Run In My Shoes is now updated after the elections of both Presidents Obama and Trump. This update is my newest attempt to educate and bring about a different perspective to the conversation about race after the Obama's 2016 termination of his terms and the new election of Trump thus far. My goal is not to attempt to add any more rhetorical and dogmatic flames to the issues of race relations, or attempting to impress readers with my writing skills, vocabulary, or even my mastery of the knowledge in which I possess in the field of study concerning African-American Studies and American History. No, my immediate strategy will be to bring about a fresh alternative approach to all learning how to "just get along". I am supporting a healing relations method by relying on sport events for the masses of citizens. The focus will be on bringing all people from both genders for play which requires no specialty skills or size needed. This would help in just bringing people together and perhaps building natural human bonds. Nothing seems to do that better than sports in America. I also do recommend my sport invention, Tagball and positive citizen workshops in order to bring as many diverse people together, thus breaking down the social and cultural barriers. I believe that by bringing the races together physically playing an easy to play sport, can help de-stress participants more rapidly, and then providing race relations seminars which can help break the ice concerning such issues as to why 70% of Americans have opinions that race and cultural relations have declined recently.

However, now regarding my present updates to Run In My Shoes update to the second edition, I have been asked to bring to my readers more personal information in this updated edition concerning my life experiences which did help to influence me in becoming so impassioned about facing racism and writing about Prejudice and Racism as topics back in the 90's and now. Originally, I intended that Run In My Shoes would have become a Pro-active message in order to stimulate rational dialog to offset the remnants of America's original sins against people of color, especially people of African origins.

In America today, we are seeing what appears to be very troubling issues regarding a negative escalation of wars, pollution, global warming, terror, mass incarceration for profit, race hatred, gang involvement, police brutality, political corruption, illegal immigration, economic decline, global nuclear proliferation, and many other social issues related to America and other countries. It appears everyone is attempting as best as they can to survive regarding the day to day issues affecting one side or the other economically, racially, and, or culturally. However, my writings and services along with other authors can perhaps present help in order to bring our planet towards a more rational focus on what we all share in common in order to bring about social and economic reforms especially between the races in America.

However, I am now going to deviate as I stated from my earlier discussions concerning racism in this present edition as well as from other immediate American and worldwide issues. I am going to now share some of my biographical highlights. Writing about self is something that I have always refrained from doing concerning Run In My Shoes. Therefore, my attempt to bring to my readers a more personalized understanding of what spiritual, environmental, and DNA factors influenced me towards my becoming dedicated to positively influencing race relations in America. My desire in giving you these autobiographical periods of my life will be to shed light on a period of great optimism, change and, yet sometimes horrific political and social missteps that appear to have caused the current negative human unrests that we witness on a day-to-day basis.

The beginning and development of my passion regarding Race relations can be attributed to the Civil Right leaders of the 60's whom were dedicated towards positive change. My growing up, living and working in communities such as, Alexandria, VA, Prince George County, MD, Washington DC, surely shaped my world, as well as some of my family, friends, and teachers. All of this social history enhanced my stimulation, and my mission in the areas of race relations and positive human character regarding peace and non-violence. The Washington DC metropolitan area, especially Alexandria, VA. proved to be very unique, even to this day regarding enhancing race relations. Most of my adult life had been living in PGC, MD. A community which opened the doors regarding my ambitions and passions in mentoring and educating youths. Therefore, I will attempt to highlight the events and memories that helped to develop me to where I am, and what I am attempting to do.

I was born on September 25th, 1957 in Old Town, Alexandria, VA. At that time, it was still a sleepy, quiet, and southern historical city atmosphere just under seven miles outside of Washington, DC. My first real memory as a child, was feeling very secure regarding almost all levels of family, neighbors, sports and recreation. Although, the neighborhood was once all white, and now it's almost that way again, when I grew up on Boyle Street, there was only one white elderly couple that remained. We all got along. Life on Boyle Street was full of lively adults, teenagers and young kids during the late 50's and 60's. I lived side-by-side to my families and other close relatives. My great-grandmother and grandmother also lived in our small townhouse home which made life quite snug. I was always the one who made a creative spot to call my sleeping quarters. However back then, nothing appeared to bother us about those types of things. We were all close, well fed, happy, and well cared for by my total extended family.

In the sixties, it seemed like almost everyone that l knew went to some kind of church on Sunday's back then, but as a side bar to my unscientific observation of attendance norms. I must note that my great-grandmother had somewhat retired from her days of church attendance moving into her eighties. She often enjoyed attending the long church camp meetings and all day church programs at Ebenezer Church, which she loved so much. Also my grandmother, my dad's mom; however, as kind as she was never routinely attended church. I always wondered back then how she could be so giving and protective, but not a consistent church goer. My mother's mom was very ill, and I never saw her well enough to go anywhere. She died very early in my life. I and most black people during that time were very influenced by the church and the preachers. My dad also did not attend Sunday services routinely on Sundays, but his cover was that he often attended church, because he was a Funeral Director. He was always in church generally. Maybe he just took Sunday's off.

A little more about dad, in addition to the chapter in book dedicated to his legacy, called, Passing the Torch. My dad was a real teacher by nature with a good heart. It just happened that he taught about Mortuary science, and his observations of life in general. My dad was also multi-talented in carpentry and electrical skills. My father was very hard working, and he and I shared many of positive days and experiences while I was under the age of (19) nineteen. After that time, we never were as close as we were then. Generally, he was very philosophical and pragmatic regarding life and race relations. It seemed like everyone knew him. Back then, an Afro-American man bringing a Cadillac limo home was still unique. The funeral business made us kind of different from the rest of the hard working neighbors. However, truly hanging around with him while he embalmed or conducted business has had a lasting impression on me, and it also made me very aware of the brevity of life.

I not only grew up influenced by him, but also my uncles and particularly my godmother and aunt, Ms. Alice Holland. My dad actually worked for my Aunt's first husband before inheriting their business, The Lewis Funeral Home. Those were the days of development, a care-free enterprise, adventures, endless play and lots of family special occasions. However, sometimes, there were moments that were laced with tense issues of negative inner family turmoil between my mother and father. They often could exhibit numerous arguments over issues like my dad's womanizing, and, or my mother hanging out too late with her sister whom appeared to me then a bad influence to my parents relationship. Back then, they and their friends could really put away the Old Grand Dad bourbon during holidays and outings. All of these highlights and more were the personal situations regarding the Bell family realities from some of my childhood memories.

While living during the Sixties was one of the most incredible periods of change and turmoil in American history with the exception of living today, and perhaps during the Civil War period. The fear then was actually like the world today since 911. The exception being, the number of physical assassinations of American leaders back then. Now instead of physical assassinations, we just seem to have endless character assassinations, mass incarcerations, and it also appears that we have far less freedoms, civil liberties, and an increased fear of police brutalities without accountability. On one hand, we also have more money in the hands of wealthy people no matter what culture or race. Some of the most notable events that happened during my early childhood were the Cuban Missile Crisis, 1968 Riots, the assassinations of President John F. Kennedy, Malcolm X, Martin Luther King, Jr., and Robert Kennedy. It was an era that many fought for improving the racial social and economic divide that was so current then and even now. It was from these great heroes of change, living next door to Washington DC, the influence of the church, and especially my love for debate that sparked my interest in wanting to pursue a different path from the mission that my dad had wanted for me towards succeeding him as his heir to the Funeral tradition that he had envisioned. He really almost had me locked down to that, but my love of sports and working with the youth turned out to become my most natural love and talent which has taken me to this time of molding my persona and ambitions.

Now for me personally, the most radical social event that would truly shape my world and totally enhanced my outlook on prejudice, race, achievement, and ambitions was attending St. Stephen's College Preparatory School. St. Stephen's began as a slow experiment towards integration before mass integration had occurred in the City of Alexandria, VA. The mass integration story was depicted in the movie "Remember the Titans". The story was about how the city coped with a larger experiment of desegregation. I will always remember the day that I visited St. Stephen's. The school was like nothing I had seen before. It reminded me of a college. My mother asked me, would I like to attend the school. I told her that I would do anything to go to the school just judging it from the outer and inner appearances. All that I was told that I needed to pass the entrance exam, and I would be eligible for a National Negro Scholarship that could help reduce the total financial burden on my parents. For those times then and now, St. Stephen's and all private IAC schools like Sidwell Friends, St. Albans, and Georgetown Prep had very expensive tuition scales. Therefore, generally, very elite and wealthy children only attended an IAC private schools. All I knew then was that I just could see me playing football, running up and down their college looking football field, fantasizing about the sport that I loved so dearly.

Oh well, I took the entrance exam, and I did not pass it. However, during the initial interview process, the Head Master of St. Stephen's, Dr. Emmet Hoy approved my acceptance. I was told that he was very impressed with my personality, and although I did not pass the academic test, he felt that I would fit socially if I would attend summer school and repeat the 5th grade in order to catch up academically. Believe it or not, I made the decision immediately upon hearing the news of how I could get into St. Stephen's. I often think back about the level of wisdom that I had regarding the decision. Most kids that I told and tell the story to say that they would not have repeated a grade. However, I knew then, and I will always know that the decision was the best for me academically and socially. It enhanced me on a pathway regarding almost everything that I encountered and has become important to me in my life.

I was the 3rd Afro-American to walk through the doors of St. Stephen's in 1967. Ironically, my cousin, Dr. Lloyd A. Lewis, the son of Aunt Alice and Uncle Butch, the founder of the Lewis Funeral Home. Lloyd Jr., Toney, as we called him, was the first to integrate St. Stephen's several years before my arrival. He was much more prepared for the studies and integration process than I was. However, almost immediately, I did excel in sports, which made me many friends socially. I continued to become a young star football standout in lower, middle and upper school as I progressed, as well as in my home community as a player, leader, team captain, and a quarterback. I was the 1st black quarterback and first black team captain to win the school inter championship regarding St. Stephen's school championship in the six grade. I also learned to gain great confidence in my studies. However, I had generally lagged behind in Latin and Math for a couple of years. It seemed like I just did not get it, but I made up for it in Summer school two straight years until I matured enough to get it during the regular school year. Socially, St. Stephen's laid the ground work for my confidence and development in dealing with the complexities of race, and it led to me becoming comfortable in my skin regarding being an Afro-American and an average economic status person living or studying around all types of people from various races, religions, and economic groups, especially the wealthy White ones. All the areas of the social experiment were covered with the exception that it did not help me at all when it came to understanding the opposite sex, but that would come later after the 10th grade by obtaining my driver's license and by then falling for my first love, April Grayson. I was fortunate to integrate into such a unique situation, in which I will always remember the school parents, and fellow classmates, like Charlie White, Lupton Abshire, Billy Babyak, Ben Jones, Randy Heflin, Randy Vosbeck,

Win Wright, Jerry Nine, and many more white classmates whom took it upon themselves to share their environments, homes and resources which truly helped to expose me to much greater situations. If I had remained at the all black St. Joseph's Catholic school, and in my neighborhood, I know now that I would not have ever been exposed to the many realities, experiences, and education that I received from St. Stephen's.

I also distinctly remember that it was the public transportation bus ride to St. Stephens and back then was also another important level of journeys and socialization. Before my attending St. Stephen's, I was use to walking to school about 10 blocks away from home with my Afro-American peers. I never had more than one white teacher my first 5 years of schooling. All of my peers and community were socio-economically the same. However, at St. Stephen's I was suddenly in a new world given the sink or swim situation regarding communicating, learning, and interacting daily. I was also counted on as a teammate in sports and even leader as a captain of students whom were from white wealth, prestige, and exclusive homes that I would sometimes think about how many times and I could have fit my house then and now into some of their mansions. The first time in the 5th grade when I really grew up to face the economic disparity was when the summer school and summer camp bus changed the route from dropping me off last to dropping me off nearly first. My environment and home life was illuminated to both my neighborhood peers and school mates of St. Stephen's. What a day that was. I went from the eyes of those classmates as being seen as one of them economically to the realities of an Afro-American living in a middle to lower socio-economic environment compared to wealthy white kids that I attended camp and school with during that period of segregation in American History. The clash of the two worlds almost sent me into negative psychological retreat never wanting to face the new reality of going back to school with my wealthy white peers exposed personally and economically. However, I conquered my insecurities and eventually grew beyond that fear.

Now the Seventies were coming along close to the late sixties when I had started to clearly remember my interest towards the political election between Hubert Humphrey, George Wallace, and Richard Nixon. Besides my many sport interactions I also carried on many religious conversations and debates between my Christian, Jewish, Humanist, Secular, and Agnostic classmates. I would have these discussions at least on a weekly basis. I was also toting the voice of what was seen from an Afro-American perspective amongst very white conservative raised classmate peers. However, I can note that it was probably then when I learned that I could not change folk, but I had come to respect their differences from someone else's perspective. It was so different from my home and most black community experiences regarding God and Christian life. In the Black community then and now, the Christian faith still remains the most important element of the moral and social fabric of the Afro-American community and experience.

Now it was about at this period, that I noted my mental growth regarding my feelings were becoming more secure with the plight of the Afro-American side of issues amongst my white peers. I was attempting to grow an Afro Bush hair style whenever I could hide long enough from my father, but the main point was that I was starting to see both Blacks and Whites more objectively, socially, and politically. In addition to the civil right changes. It was also the period where the early Seventies were bringing in the Motown sounds and images. This era was captivating me and most black youths. We became more and more very interested in physically identifying with groups racially and socially like the Jackson 5, and television weekly music show, the Soul Train. Had it not been for these very images, I may have absorbed only an all White world of imagery, behaviors, and social perspectives.

Also, during this period, I noted that being a football leader was still there, but my position was changing. A tall blond white kid, Kendall Hayes, whom I really liked a lot as a fellow classmate and sport peer was named QB and not me for the following season. I was a shorter, but more elusive kid. I had an outstanding football IQ and I could scramble well. I was more in the image like a Fran Tarkenton, Mike Vic, and the Russel Wilson types. However, I learned to enjoy playing the left corner back spot. I also played running back as well. Now at this stage of my life as an adolescent, my love for competition was being measured against the schools with greater sport reputations, and Afro-American players it seemed like. That way of seeing things made me believe that I needed to leave the school in which I stated made so much of a difference on my physical, sociological, and psychological development. Now this drive for sport recognition became the backdrop of all the positive soulful changes that were happening to me, and my love for being considered one of the best football players in the city of Alexandria did cause me to attend another all-white boys preparatory school named Bishop Ireton. My desire to play in the elite private school Metro conference was more important to me over friends at St. Stephens. The Metro conference then and today is conference known for outstanding teams and players. St. Stephen's was still more of the academically, holistic, well rounded, nice guy school image conference in the way that I looked at it at that time.

When I started Bishop Ireton, I was not really prepared for the differences socially. Yes, it was also still mostly white and wealthy, but there were at least 15 other Afro-American students besides myself. However, Ireton kids were a lot more tribal than the students at St. Stephen's. It was very Catholic. However, besides sports, I did love the religion classes and debates. I also really became much more confident academically. I was even hanging tough among the Math guys. I also began to excel in basketball, and decided to lay off a year to see where the football team was headed although the coach was always trying to get me on the team. However, I went the way of basketball. The basketball experience was good and bad in some ways, and I did get the competition levels that I was seeking, however I did not really fit in socially, as well as I did at St. Stephen's in some very distinctive ways. Also, during this time my parent's marriage was also coming unglued. I kind of took advantage of that pressure. I now had my eyes on leaving Ireton. They had already objected to me leaving St. Stephens, and now, a year later, I wanted to leave Ireton for an even bigger sport name in Alexandria City football, T.C. Williams High School. The strain on their marriage made it easier for me to make the change.

Now for a bit of a backdrop for you the reader concerning living in the prime of the seventies. As far as I have seen life as an African-American, it appears to me that living during the seventies was the most racially harmonious period in America. In addition, I now realize that I experienced living in Alexandria personally, was one of America's greatest racial integration success stories to this day compared to many others US cities and states. I do not think it was a coincidence that I grew up with such great passion and love for people, because I lived in one of the most progressive cities in America that truly worked on racial integration. The movie, "Remember the Titans' if you've seen it, surely depicted the realities of how folk made change racially. It also helps to visualize the words that I am writing concerning my passion concerning race relations.

Okay, all three schools that I attended in Alexandria had shaped my early development. My high school graduation was in 1976, The Bicentennial Birthday of the United States of America. All I had on my mind at that time was working with my dad in the Funeral business, a civil rights ministry, my friends, interest sports, and going to a predominantly historical colleges like Morehouse or Howard University to pursue my ambitions. This again is the backdrop for you the reader concerning living during the awesome seventies in America. Before graduation, I did not even play football or basketball my senior year at TC. I attributed it to having more interests in social and academic pursuits going to a co-educational school versus the all-male schools like St. Stephen's and Bishop Ireton. I had also become disenchanted with the realities of football politics, and the wear and tear on body at TC at the time. I found myself becoming more interested in working in the funeral business with my dad, school debates, girls, and where I ultimately would attend college. My intellectual curiosity really stood out as well. I was a combination black minister and a hippy teenager. All of the major stories and headlines regarding black people, Watergate and Richard Nixon were heavy on my mind. Most of my peers were really confused about my stances, but I can say with great clarity looking back that I was a peace seeking youth looking for the answers. People whom were very important to me were my Close Friends, like Al Hayes, Steve Johnson, Sewel Johnson, Aunt Alice, family and my girlfriend April Grayson, later to become my wife in the eighties.

My desire to become a Minister/Philosopher like that of the model of Dr. King really became very important to me just as much as working with my dad and all of the other social activities that I shared with friends and girlfriend. I had applied to three universities, I finally selected Howard University. My college experiences were of great influence. Howard University turned out to be a good start towards my social and political levels of my college experience. However, not so good for my academic side. DC was in close proximity to many diversions like dad, friends, and just a lot of overall social distractions for a popular freshmen youth. After two years of it, I ended up on academic probation.

During my academic probation, I came to a personal relation spiritually with Christ and with other great teachers whom were spiritually based. I was heavily influenced by Christ, and I considered myself as Christ centered. I also began to cleanse my mind and body from many of the social distractions at the time. I started to work out daily, often running ten miles or more, and reading, as well as working with my dad. I was a new person. I had given up on becoming so socially down for all of the parties and trips to have social fun. After one year on probation at Howard, I had re-applied and was accepted back to Howard. However, a series of changes including going to be with the lady that I loved landed me at Cheyney University until a major car accident occurred injuring me greatly then causing my return to Maryland to finish up my education at Bowie State University.

During the Bowie State years and after graduation from there, my wife and I worked for my dad, the Prince George's County (PGC) school system, Fairfax County recreation system and started a lawn service. After an accident to my wife's hand changing a bag on a mower, we folded all belongings up and we went to Salisbury NC, where I was accepted to Hood Theological Seminary. It was here where the greatest emotional challenge occurred in my life. The woman that I loved so much could not keep our marriage together. After this episode, I left NC, and I finally started my MA all over again in what has developed into my passion for developing strategies and programs for improving black achievement, peace and race relations in America. Now I am going to conclude this chapter by saying it is my desire that one day, I can say that I have taken on the legacies of Christ, Dr. King, my dad, and so many others in teaching how to improve and overcome whatever gets in the way regarding health and peace on this planet.

ABOUT THE AUTHOR

by D'Andrea Brown

Phillip Bell was born on September 25th, 1957 at Freemans Hospital in Washington, D.C. His earliest memories were those of a young child growing up on Boyle Street in Alexandria, Virginia. A middle child between two sisters, Phillip was a mischievous prankster. It was not unusual for a babysitter to refuse to return after being locked in a closet. He was just as well known for his compassionate side. At age eight he rescued a neighbor, Elizabeth Mckenzie, who had fallen during a winter storm. She had slipped and fallen on the icy steps during the night, and Phillip responded to her weak cries for help. Her husband, Mr. Mack, worked at night, and if Phillip had not discovered her, she may have lain there until morning. Fortunately, she was able to return home after a short hospital stay. Phillip was a favored child among friends and family. From a very early age Phillip's parents expected great things of him.

Phillip was born into a lower middle class family where both parents worked to provide as best they could for the three siblings. Phillip Bell, Sr. was an ex-military man who worked his way through mortuary school and became one of the first black business owners in Alexandria. Phillip Bell, Senior encouraged all of his children to work in the family business. Phillip's older sister, Winona worked in the business to a minimal extent only when she reached her teens. His younger sister Anita, escaped the experience all together. As the only son, Phillip felt the greatest pressure to follow in his father's footsteps.

From as early as the age of eight his father began training him in the funeral business. He began his training by cleaning and answering phones and worked his way through to transporting bodies with their families in the company hearses. His first assignment, to retrieve a body from D.C. Morgue, was in 1974 at the age of seventeen years. It was a bloody, gruesome experience. Unclaimed cadavers from the 1968 race riots where still there along with the mutilated bodies of the more recently departed. Some bodies were decapitated, some hacked up, and still others wore facial expressions that reflected the terror of their impending demise. Caught totally unprepared for this scene, Phillip struggled to keep from passing out. This scene was more ghastly than that of any horror movie he has seen from that day to present. Undoubtably, Phillip's early exposure to the reality of human mortality shaped his views on physical fitness and gave him a greater appreciation for the days that we are granted to spend on this earth.

The Bell family business grew and gained prominence in Alexandria. Throughout childhood and as a young adult, the family business would allow Phillip to rub shoulders with the most affluent people of his time. He attended funeral director's conventions in various cities hobnobbing with the wealthy. From ages sixteen to twenty he chauffeured many celebrities and social activist such as Lou Gossett, Jr., Reverend Jessie Jackson, and Laura and Pam Brown. It was these early experiences along with the social climate of the time that gave him his first glimpse of race relations in America. His educational experiences were the most tangible source for development of his prospective on problems between the races. At that time, although not a new concept, integration was at the infancy stages of actualization.

Phillip's mother, Phyllis Bell, was a natural educator who strove to give her children the best academic and moral education within the family's means. She enrolled the children in area private schools. At the elementary level Phillip attended St. Joseph's, an all black Catholic school. Mrs. Bell also worked in the school system where she met and became friends with Ms. Eddie. Ms. Eddie was a school administrator who was a proponent of logically progressive integration. She encouraged Mrs. Bell to apply for Phillip's enrollment in St. Stephen's, a white parochial school that was interviewing possible candidates for integration. The Bell family was acquainted with the integration process and had an idea of what to expect from the ordeal. Phillip's cousin had been the first black to integrate St. Stephen's a couple of years prior.

Phillip was a very gregarious child, and it was his personality that gave him the edge that he needed to gain acceptance into St. Stephen's. During his time there Phillip's instructors and friends would play an important role in his adjustment to cultural differences and reactions to integration. At St. Stephen's, Phillip's athletic potential was recognized and cultivated. Throughout his athletic career he would continue to develop the principles of his style of leadership. He became a well-touted athlete at St. Stephen's participating in their football program. But even sportsmanship was not enough to supersede the racial divisions of the times.

On several occasions to away games in black neighborhoods racial tensions escalated to the point of near disaster. On one occasion the St. Stephen's team bus was barraged with shouts of racial slurs. As black students from nearby schools shook the bus, the fearful Stephen's students inside dawned all of their protective gear from helmets to knee pads to prepare for what they were sure would end in a bloody assault. Unsure as to whether or not his skin color would be enough to save him from the raft of his assailants, Phillip too was terrified. The St. Stephens coach shouted reassuring words to his team in an attempt to calm them. Thankfully, the incident ended with the safe return of the students to St. Stephens. Phillip witnessed many such incidents which reinforced how crucial it is to keep a calm head in the face of chaos. It was the discipline and camaraderie of team sports that proved to be a major factor in overcoming many racial barriers encountered throughout Phillip's life.

His participation in sports continued on through high school where he played basketball at Bishop Ireton. While Phillip was growing up, professional sports remained a frontier for Blacks. But as he matured the world of sports would undergo its own evolutionary process. Phillip contemplated the trail blazing accomplishments of Black athletes . . . Jackie Robinson breaking the color barrier in baseball, Muhammad Ali's triumph over Sonny Liston, and many others. These tremendous athletes helped to reinforce his great love and respect for sports.

Phillip also witnessed the ugly side of the power and passion behind these social changes. His childhood was scattered with memories of the tumultuous times in which he grew. After the assassination of Dr. Martin Luther King, Jr., race riots erupted. From across the Potomac River in Alexandria, he watched the smoke rise from the fires in the streets of Washington, DC. Along with many other families the Bells turned on their porch lights. The word was spread through the neighborhood that the lights would indicate they were Black or "had soul" and were to be left alone. A symbolic gesture similar to the biblical account of the Jewish Passover.

Of paramount importance in his development was Phillip's belief in God. While his education at St. Josephs provided a rudimentary understanding of religion, the variety of religious backgrounds and encouragement of open discussion at St. Stephens brought fundamental spiritual principles to life for Phillip. The experience was so enlightening that Jesus became, and remains to this day, the most influential person in Phillip's life. Phillip's inquisitive nature led him to his desire for a better understanding of this man Jesus. He often pondered the incarnation and eternal nature of Jesus. He viewed Jesus as a spiritual revolutionary who, unlike others before or since him, was able to bypass the superficial and get to the essence. Other biblical persons that influenced Phillip were Samson, David, and Moses men of great strength and humility.

The religious values Phillip had learned would be reinforced and demonstrated through the life examples that his great-grandmother, Grandma Theresa, and grandmother, Grandma Talley, provided. Grandma Talley had a special place in her heart for Phillip. She took to calling him Lamby, a term of endearment the she uses to this day. Grandma Theresa was a peaceful and godly woman. She was the closest person, to what Phillip believed Jesus to be like, that he had ever met. Grandma Talley and Grandma Theresa saw to the day-to-day needs of the household and gave the children the extra love and spiritual fortitude they would need to make it through the difficult times.

Many of Phillip's family members played a significant role in his development. He remembers fondly the kindness and love shown by his Aunt Alice, Aunt Mary and Uncle Ferris. His older sister Winona, even as a young woman, was pretty, intelligent, and socially polished. She helped to guide him through the pitfalls of puberty. She advised him on the potentially destructive results of teen fatherhood and encouraged him to focus on academics. Their mother, being the shrewd woman that she was, capitalized on their great friendship by sending Phillip along with Winona as chaperone to social events. As they grew older the time came for them to take their separate paths in life. Through the customary fallouts of brother and sister, divorces, and tough times their friendship remains.

After graduating from high school Philip attended Howard University and Cheyney State College before earning a Bachelor of Arts degree in Psychology from Bowie State University. Phillip went on to earn a Master of Arts degree in African-American Studies from Vermont College. Out of his love of sports and compassion for children Phillip was compelled to establish Bell/Metropolitan Educational Achievement Club. His organization has helped many children, that would have otherwise fallen through the cracks, to become productive members of society. He is now a behavioral engineer, businessman, inventor, educator, actor, and entrepreneur. In the same spirit of the many great men and women before him, Phillip continues to strive toward excellence in his accomplishments in his business and personal endeavors. His greatest desire is to leave a legacy that will inspire, to even greater achievements, those he will leave behind.

Phillip Bell, Jr.

Phyllis Bell, Anita, Phillip Bell, Sr., and Winona (left to right)

Phillip at age 8

Phillip in Jr. High School Years

Phillip at Bishop Ireton High School

**Cake from a celebration at Thomas Jefferson where
Phillip's elementary education began**

Phillip Bell, Jr. - 1991

Phillip Bell, Jr. - 1985

**Wes Unseld, Former Baltimore/Washington Bullets was
Commencement Address Speaker at Phillip's Graduation
from Bowie State University®**

Phillip, 2nd from bottom right, at St. Stephens, Seminary Road, Alexandria, Virginia

Phillip Bell Jr., is the 4th from the left at Bishop Ireton High School, Alexandria, Virginia

Phillip Bell., Sr.

**Phillip Sr., Graduation
Parker-Gray Alexandria, VA**

Phillip Bell, Sr., US Army

Passing the Torch

The Story of One Man's Legacy
by
D'Andrea Brown
Content Editing by Phillip Bell, Jr.
Technical Editing by Lauren A. Ransom

Building a legacy is often a part of the human quest for the meaning of life as well as an attempt to immortalize ones self. The achievements and contributions of many great men and women in American history are well documented in historical text. But what of the lesser known Americans who have had a tremendous impact on our society and culture: the unsung heroes who affect our lives on a smaller scale but with no lesser significance than those we read about in American history? Phillip Bell, Jr. and Phillip Bell, Sr. are examples of two such men: great American heroes whose song also deserves to be sung. The biography of Phillip Bell, Sr. is an illustration of how one man, against great odds, passed on courage and compassion to his son which has allowed him to make a significant impact on our ever-evolving society.

Alexandria, Virginia, home to this country's founding father, was also home to Phillip Bell, Jr. and Phillip Bell, Sr. This city, with its rich history, has all the milieu of a bustling political town and yet still reserves its small town feel. Phillip Bell, Jr. and Phillip Bell, Sr., shared in the richness of Alexandria's diverse cultures, economic opportunities, and social struggles over two generations. Although they chose seemingly diverse careers, their motives and aspirations were very similar. The experiential parallels in their lives were strikingly similar up until their teens, but to this day they still share many of the same principles that lead them to most of their life choices.

Phillip Bell, Sr. has been a mortician and funeral director for the past 30 years; choosing to care for and comfort those at the end-of-life process. Whereas Phillip Bell, Jr. has chosen to counsel and nurture those at the beginning of life, children. They both saw the need and had the desire to positively impact their social environment. Surely, not many African-American men of Phillip Bell, Sr.'s time just awoke one morning overcome with the urge to surround themselves with death and grieving. So why did he choose mortuary science? Perhaps the decision to become involved in the funeral industry was partially due to the limited business opportunities that existed at that time for African-American males to become both wealthy and to be a humanitarian. Rather than making assumptions about his career choice, I decided to go straight to the source. The response from Phillip Bell Sr. took me on a colorful journey through African-American History and one man's story of his development into manhood.

Phillip Bell, Sr. was born in Washington, DC on April 9, 1932. He grew up in Alexandria during a time when the city was much more rural. He recalls living at 321 South Alfred Street near a neighborhood store where the owner kept horses behind the store in a make shift barn. At that time there were no ordinances against keeping horses in the city and young Phillip Bell, Sr. worked in the store and also fed and cared for the horses in the mornings before going to school. So began his involvement with horses and association with the white, prominent families in the community. These families took a personal interest in him and on Sundays he began to travel with them to public and private horse shows such as those held at the Herby's (of Herby's Ford) farm in Franconia. He became well respected for his work ethic and skill. By age 13 or 14 he became an English style horseman and began working for these families caring for, jumping and breaking horses. He even broke a wild colt that became a professional prize winning racehorse called Dress Parade.

Because Phillips relationships with these affluent families went beyond business associations, they often went as friends to other public affairs and social gatherings. Alexandria, at this time, was segregated, and Phillip Bell, Sr. was very conspicuous among these older white males. Phillip recounts the tension and opposition he and his friends encountered when entering segregated establishments. Being men of substantial influence in the community, his friends would state, in no uncertain terms, their expectations for Phillip to be regarded as one of them. Paradoxically, these same friends often referred to other African-Americans as niggers and used other derogatory terms to describe African-Americans in Phillip's presence. It was as if they did not recognize Phillip's race and so felt at ease using these terms without fear of offending him. One thing is certain, the whole issue of race did not stand in the way of Phillip's friendship with his wealthy white mentors. Taken under the wing of these accomplished business men, Phillip learned many of the skills that would later assist him in becoming a successful businessman in his own right.

Phillip's exposure to the funeral business began very early. He lived near a business that made and sold tombstones, Chancey's Monument Shop. Phillip worked at Chancey's as early as the age of 7 or 8, assisting with placing markers on graves and trimming the grass around the stones. More practical exposure was provided by his uncle, Lloyd A. Lewis. Lloyd Lewis was one of the first African-American funeral directors in the District of Columbia. He established his funeral home in 1927 and was one of the most prominent African-American men in the DC metropolitan area. By the age of 14 Phillip was assisting his uncle in the business by helping to transport bodies, embalming, and taking care of the cars and equipment. This was the era of Studebakers, Packards, and Chrysler limousines. In those days, most of the embalming and services were held in the family's homes or in churches. It wasn't until later that these procedures took place at funeral homes. Among other duties, Phillip was responsible for maintaining the coach boards, which contained the rubber sheets, buckets for blood, and other items used for the embalming process. He recalls disposing of the waste from embalming done in homes by flushing it down the toilet. Phillip would later draw on these experiences to make his way through the highs and lows that he would encounter. His friends, family and many others in his community would all contribute to his success.

The earliest influences in his life were those of his mother and grandparents. Phillip grew up in a single-parent household with extended family. His grandfather was an interesting character who was an entrepreneur in his time. Sebraun Bell was a shoe repairman by day and worked for a florist at night. Sebraun also trapped and skinned animals in his spare time, selling the pelts to furriers. His mother, Talley, was a hard working, strong, and independent woman who did days work in various places, from private homes to beauty shops. His grandmother, Theresa, also did domestic work. Phillip remembers his grandmother as being a very outgoing woman who had a talent for communicating with those of all ages. It was Theresa that gave Phillip his nickname, Chick, which she ascribed to him because as a newborn he was very tiny. His Godmother, Mellisa Cross, was a midwife who delivered many of the babies born in their neighborhood. Ms. Cross lived next door and baby-sat Phillip. She often stepped in to rescue Phillip when his mother scolded him for ruining his clothes in horseplay with other boys. She also took Phillip along with her to a local Methodist Church on some Sundays. Ms. Cross was great fun and a very creative sitter. Once she even tied a string around a chicken's neck as a makeshift leash and allowed Phillip to walk the chicken like a dog. When going to deliver babies, Ms. Cross carried a large, brown pocketbook. Phillip accompanied Ms. Cross on some of her visits to do infant care. Seeing the two together, on lookers would comment that the pair was bringing yet another baby in her big, brown pocketbook. Phillip has many fond memories of his family and friends.

One of Phillip's closest friends, Clayton Thompson (Bunny), has been in his life since early childhood, and they remains close to this day. Phillip recalls how he and Bunny shared an interest in horses and went where they could to be around them. Phillip's interest in horses and his involvement with friends who owned horses took up a great deal of his time. Bunny, who was a less serious horseman, sometimes stayed behind choosing other pursuits. Phillip and Bunny joke now about how Bunny stole his teenage sweetheart while Phillip was otherwise occupied. Bunny eventually married the girl and they had twelve children together. Bunny's wife is deceased, but Phillip and Bunny's friendship continues on, and they often reminisce about the good old days.

Phillip attended Lyles Crouch Elementary School, and Parker Grey Middle and High School in Alexandria. Phillip, who was very popular in school, was president of the student body and also played the trumpet and French horn in the school band. He credits his high school shop teacher, Mr. Authur Bracey, as being a great influence in his life. Under Mr. Bracey's tutelage, Phillip learned the skills that would allow him to do electrical work and carpentry to support himself and his family while establishing his career as a funeral director and mortician. Through unforeseen circumstances and an unlikely turn of events, Phillip would be edged further down his career path.

In 1950, North Korea, seeking to achieve Korean unification under Communist rule, invaded South Korea. Harry S. Truman, President of the United States at the time, reacted by sending troops to support South Korean ground units. Thus began America's involvement in the Korean War.[1] By this time, Phillip Bell, Sr. had just graduated from high school. Only a couple of months prior he had turned 18 years of age and was eligible for the draft. However, it wasn't until 1952 that his number came up and he was drafted into the United States Army. For the first time in the history of the United States of American troops would be integrated. Desegregation of the United States military could not have come at a better time for Phillip. He would now have the educational opportunities that had never been extended to African-American soldiers. Phillip underwent eight weeks of basic training in Augusta, GA. He was then transferred to Ft. Monmouth in New Jersey, where he was interviewed to receive an assignment. Because of his experience in the funeral business he was assigned to the army's grave registration unit. He was eventually stationed at Governor's Island. He began working at a medical lab on 90 Church Street in Manhattan, New York. His first assignment was to work in the mailroom where specimens were received and shipped for testing. Samples of food products were also received to ensure that they met military standards. Phillip then rotated through the serology lab, there he performed the test necessary for his own marriage license. He went on through the chemistry lab and finally ended up in pathology were he processed tissue specimens with sources ranging from surgery to autopsy.

In 1953, Phillip was transferred to Walter Reed in Washington, DC where he worked in the experimental surgery section of their pathology lab. Many soldiers were lost due to injuries, which irreparably damaged the aorta. Injury to the aorta, being the largest artery in the body, meant certain death. Repair of the aorta was beyond the scope of medical technology, and experiments were conducted on various methods of repair. Phillip recalls the experiment that involved patching the aorta with different types of materials. At one point they also attempted to the repairs with arteries from chimpanzees. The cost of one chimpanzee at the time was $600. The military eventually found this to be too costly and abandoned them using pigs instead that were raised at Forest Glenn. Experiments with tissue from the pigs proved to be more cost effective since they could also use the meat remaining for food.

In mid-1953, a truce agreement ended the Korean War.[2] Phillips's military career was over, but he was still too young to become a funeral director. Since he was not yet 21, he was not eligible to enter into legal agreements and the contracts that would be necessary for funeral directorship. At that time an embalmer's license and funeral director's license were awarded separately. Phillip enrolled in the American Academy of Funeral Service in Manhattan, New York, on Broadway. He graduated in 1955 and returned to Alexandria for two years of internship in his uncle's business. In 1957 he applied for and was awarded his embalmer's license. He continued to work in his uncles business and began doing trade embalming for various funeral homes. Shortly thereafter he obtained his funeral director's license.

Fully licensed and with a number of years of experience under his belt, Phillip sought to purchase property were he could begin his own business. On February 28, 1952, Phillip married Phyllis Diggs, who worked in the Alexandria public school system. Phyllis was a no nonsense, outgoing woman who worked alongside her husband to help provide for their family. The couple moved to South Alfred Street with their three young children. Finding the house overrun with rodents, Phillip Bell, Sr. was determined to move his family into a safer environment. As a result he worked long hours and spent time with his children by enlisting them to work in his business. Phillip's first child, Winona, only later in life took interest, and his youngest daughter, Anita, did not even pretend to be interested in learning the funeral business. Phillip had high hopes that his second born would become more involved. Phillip Bell, Sr.'s greatest aspiration for his son was that he would adopt his father's entrepreneurial spirit and the life skills that would enable him to be successful as well. Phillip Bell, Jr. performed many of the duties in his father's business that Phillip Sr. himself had performed growing up.

Political and social upheaval in America during the 1960s would bring tragedy and triumph to the Nation and affect both the poor and prosperous. The Bell family, caught up in the swirl of a culture in transition held on for what proved to be a roller coaster of social change. In November 1960, John

F. Kennedy became the youngest president ever elected to the United States Government. During his term in office as president, Kennedy encountered the continuance of a number of both domestic and international problems.[3] The civil rights struggle in America raged on and clashes between police and demonstrating African-Americans induced him to push civil rights legislation banning discrimination and fostering desegregation. Both he and Martin Luther King, Jr., leader of the Civil Rights Movement, would meet violent ends signaling the turmoil in America.[4] Phillip Bell, Sr. was a first-hand witness to the fall out from violence occurring in those days of civil conflict. Burying those who fell victim to the outbreak of social tensions made a lasting impression. Along with the civil conflict, America faced international problems that threatened her security. In October 1962, President Kennedy announced that Soviet atomic missile sites were being built in Cuba. This event, known as the Cuban Missile Crisis, refocused the nation's attention, bringing terror and uncertainty about the future safety and survival of America.[5]

The Bell family, also engulfed in this time of tragedy, sought to live out what may have been their last days as fully as possible. For the moment the worry over debt and day-to-day struggle was abandoned. The family indulged themselves. The children were even given toys that the family would not normally be able to afford. But this indulgence soon ended along with the Cuban Missile Crisis in November 1962. [6] The crisis passed, the Bell family along with the rest of the nation sighed in relief. Their moment of exhalation was short lived as devastating tragedy struck at the heart of the American people with the assassination of John F. Kennedy, Martin Luther King, Jr., and Robert Kennedy. Phillip recalls his participation in Robert Kennedy's funeral procession and regards it to have been a great honor. Throughout the 1960s, Phillip continued to work hard gaining more skill and knowledge with each passing year, using his carpentry and funeral business skills to support his family.

As Phillip Bell, Sr. searched for a location to begin his own business, his uncle became ill and required surgery. Knowing that the odds for surviving the surgery were slim, Mr. Lewis had his will drawn up. Unfortunately, Phillip's uncle, Lewis, never made it off of the operating table, but with the forethought of a good businessman he had made the proper arrangements for Alexandria, Virginia's oldest, African-American owned business, established in 1927, to continue. To this day the business is still in existence. There is no other business of any kind bearing the same name that has been in existence for a longer period of time. Uncle Lewis entrusted his prized life's work to someone who had proven to be both worthy and capable, Phillip Bell, Sr. Phillip, Sr. was anxious to make good on his predecessor's confidence in him. He mourned and buried his mentor. Carrying the mantel of this great man would be a challenge, but Phillip graciously accepted the challenge.

Initially, business was slow, and the family tightened their belts and supported one another. At the time it seemed as though the business would come to a complete halt. Noting his father's dejected mood and the heaviness of the Bell household; it was Phillip Jr. who led the family in prayer for the businesses to thrive. Miraculously, that same evening, the business phone began to ring and has not stopped since.

Since then Phillip Bell, Sr. has spearheaded many business-related enterprises. He attends conventions and seminars throughout the years continuing to expand and stay abreast of current advances in his field. Phillip and his partners have most recently established a new location for a funeral home that will bear his name in the Temple Hills, Maryland, area. His next goal is to own and operate a cemetery. He once owned Forest Hill Cemetery, which he purchased and then sold for a profit in less than one year. His daughter, Winnona, is now a licensed mortician and occasionally worked with her father in his business. Phillip realized his greatest desire for his son in that Phillip, Jr. has become an entrepreneur with a successful business of his own. Father and son often discuss business ideas and strategies. Although Phillip Bell, Sr. concedes that he is older, he now posses greater wisdom and his compassion for the grieving has not waned. He is now a seasoned entrepreneur and an exceptional businessman who has earned his place among those who served as his mentors.

1. Compton's Interactive Encyclopedia.Copyright 1994.1995 Compton's NewMedia, Inc.The Korean War.

2. Compton's Interactive Encyclopedia.Copyright 1994.1995 Compton's NewMedia, Inc. The Korean War

3. Compton's Interactive Encyclopedia.Copyright 1994.1995 Compton's NewMedia, Inc. Kennedy

4. Compton's Interactive Encyclopedia.Copyright 1994.1995
    Compton's NewMedia, Inc. Kennedy
5. Compton's Interactive Encyclopedia.Copyright 1994.1995
    Compton's NewMedia, Inc. Cuban Missile Crisis
6. Compton's Interactive Encyclopedia.Copyright 1994.1995
    Compton's NewMedia, Inc. Cuban Missile Crisis

A Mother's Prospective

by

Phyllis M. Bell

My son's book on race relations and his efforts to understand and ease the prejudices plaguing us today are commendable. I understand that hostility, racial prejudice, and bigotry are alive and well in America. As Phillip Jr's mother, and also a student of the bible, he asked me to comment on my thoughts following the "911" attack.

I, Phyllis M. Bell, was born in Alexandria, Virginia on October 22, 1935. Both my mother, Lucille Diggs, and grandmother, Jacquelyn Diggs, were born in Alexandria. I married Phillip Bell, Sr. in 1953. From that union three children were born: Winona Bell, now Winona Morrissette-Johnson, Phillip Bell, Jr., and Anita Bell. I also have three grand children, Monique Bell, Wesley Morrissette, and Aly Johnson.

I recently graduated from Washington Bible College. As a result of my theological training on prophecy and biblical providence, many things have been revealed to me.

There are evil forces and struggles that we don't understand nor prevent. Events such as the "911" attack, change in weather patterns, violence, wars, terrorism, earthquakes, the HIV virus, and even the presidential election for power suggest that the ancient prophecies are accurate and are being revealed exactly as prophesied. We now see plummeting morality and vastly increased travel and education that was also foretold. Man's increase in knowledge can be compared and traced to the "Tower of Babel". God stepped in and confounded the languages of men to prevent the Babylonian builders from partaking of the power and glory that belonged only to Him. We know that Iraq is the modern day Babylon, the name being change in 1958. This is another example of humanity's misguided efforts at self-glorification. When the World Trade Center collapsed, many major corporations collapsed. The purpose of the attack was to destroy the American economy and whatever represented or symbolized this country's prosperity. These events should let us know that the return of Jesus Christ is near.

In conclusion, I feel that many of us are buying into a false system, and man is seeking political power at any cost. Man may be developing weapons of mass destruction, but I personally don't believe that he will completely destroy this world. The first time God destroyed it, he said that it would be by fire the next time. The events that have recently happened did draw many people back to Christ and the church. Are we ignoring the signs of the time? Will it be possible to beat the "666" system? I feel that the "666" system is already in place in the world with everything being computerized. I pray that we heed the warning signs spoken of in the bible and also that this book has the effect that my son desires.

Author's Points Of Concern Post 911

By Phillip Bell, Jr.

I'd like to share some points of view in order to help clarify my spiritual, and geo-social/political concerns since post 911 events and issues, and how I feel events pertain to the furtherance (of a good towards) non-violence and a breakdown of prejudice and racism in America; and possibly in other regions of the world. As a lifelong advocate of education, positive behavior, and non-violent approaches to our multi-cultural differences of family, community, and American society in general, I see on our horizon an omnivorous change of American behavior since 911.

Although my position is not intended to cause political shifts in America, it is intended to stimulate many Americans to openly communicate on worldwide issues and perceptions beyond what they see on C-Span or CNN. Sectional discussions of Americans who are labeled right or left are usually due to agreement or disagreement, or national policies of political affiliations. This is a healthy way of improving our democratic republic.

I am an independent, politically minded, thinking individual steering hopefully from sometimes misguided opinions that are more affiliated with special interest concerns. What is really healthier and conducive for the environment, peace, and unity through America, and the global populations are in my foremost thoughts.

Most Americans rely on media news views and propaganda which try not to offend one with the true side of American and global concerns. I truly suggest that Americans need to work more on prayer, independent news, exercise, and positive non-violent approaches to solving differences. What we now see are acts of an emotional world apparently bent on an eye for an eye, punish them all and don't forget, let's lock up and destroy all that disagree with you. I'm not at all advocating passiveness; just the contrary. I'm advocating a strong, honest and imagined diplomacy backed with a needed response that's fair and as non-lethal to America and to the rest of the world.

Apparently, most of the problems of America, the lack of trust in our leadership, etc., can be linked to the cause and effects of historical prejudicial viewpoints and politics despite the inclusive spiritual language of the American Constitution. The American Constitution, which is the global structure of positive democracy worldwide, still fears others of special interest groups dominating political parties. Our slanted and stilted broadcast news will continue to help the perpetuation of mistrust, fears and disunity among Americans and our global neighbors.

Apparently, there is a group of disenchanted people who are not dissatisfied with simply handling the threats perceived by America's diversity. Therapies and remedies toward positive reconstruction is what is needed now. Threats of terror, as we strive to live amongst each other in this world, still consist of racial, religious, and alien cultural diversity that are the basis of all fears.

We cannot, and should not, allow forces to escalate to the leveling fears of nuclear proliferation as it was during the cold war. We must make every effort to advance the human population to handle our differences and battles without the possibility of global annihilation. This final solution, without any possible winner, is not normal global behavior. Imagine World War III being fought as a paintball game instead of with nuclear weapons?

If we could change our perception of conflict, war, and resolution . . .

Mr. & Mrs. Phillip and Phyllis Bell, Sr.

**Phillip Bell Sr., Graduate
Mortician and Funeral Director**

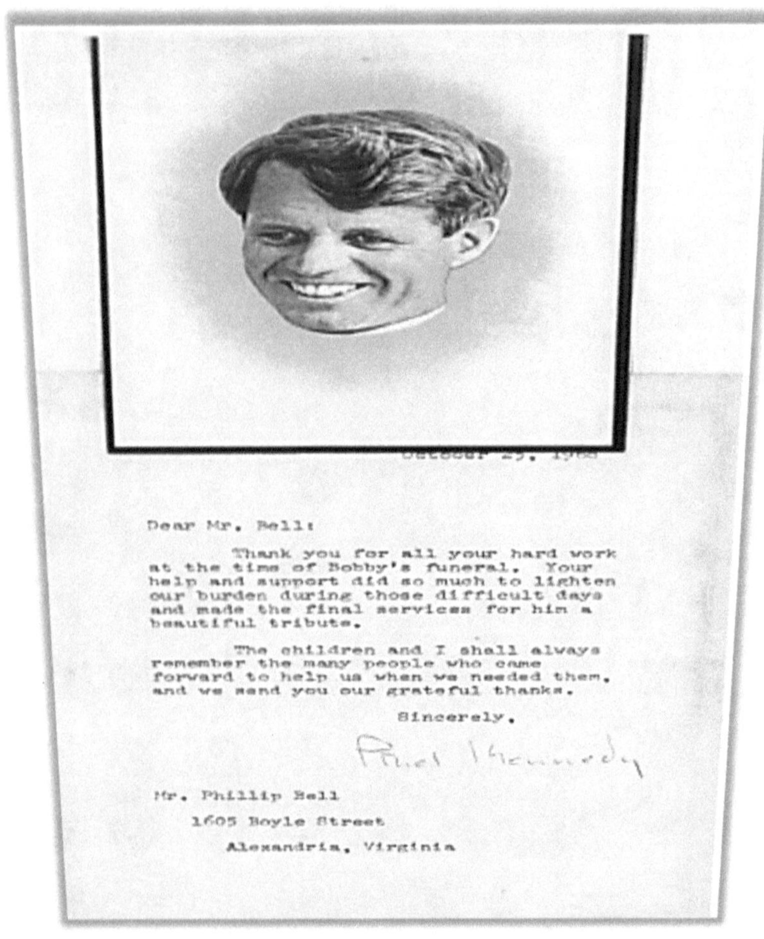

October 25, 1968

Dear Mr. Bell:

Thank you for all your hard work at the time of Bobby's funeral. Your help and support did so much to lighten our burden during those difficult days and made the final services for him a beautiful tribute.

The children and I shall always remember the many people who came forward to help us when we needed them, and we send you our grateful thanks.

Sincerely,

Ethel Kennedy

Mr. Phillip Bell
1605 Boyle Street
Alexandria, Virginia

President John F. Kennedy
Funeral Appreciation Letter

Phyllis Bell's and Diamond, her Akita-Chow

My Nephew and Niece

The Diggs Sisters/My Aunts

Phyllis Bell, Administrative Secretary at Francis Hammond, Alexandria Virginia School System

Phyllis Diggs-Bell Wedding with Sisters

152

PLACEHOLDER BELL FAMILY

Harlem Hell Cats

Black Pioneers

Charity Early

Black Pioneers

Mohammad Ali/Dr. King

Harlem Parade

Mass Incarceration

Harriet Tubman

William Still

HARRIET TUBMAN: Harvey, Lindsley B. "[Harriet Tubman, Full-Length Portrait, Standing with Hands on Back of a Chair]." *Home*, 1 Jan. 1871, www.loc.gov/pictures/item/2003674596/

INCARCERATION: Beer, Todd. "MASS INCARCERATION: DATA, TRENDS, AND COMPARISON - Sociology Toolbox." *Sociology Toolbox MASS INCARCERATION DATA TRENDS AND COMPARISON Comments*, 17 June 2014, thesocietypages.org/toolbox/mass-incarceration/

CHARITY EARLEY-PIONEER: "Charity Earley Pioneered Black Women in the Mililtary." *African American Registry*, aaregistry.org/story/charity-earley-pioneered-black-women-in-the-mililtary/

MASS INCARCERATION: Toobin, Jeffrey. "The Milwaukee Experiment: What Can One Prosecutor Do about the Mass Incarceration of African-Americans?" *The New Yorker* , 11 May 2015, www.newyorker.com/magazine/2015/05/11/the-milwaukee-experiment.

CIVIL RIGHTS AND UNITED STATES PRESIDENTS: "Civil Rights Movement." *John F. Kennedy Presidential Library and Museum*, www.jfklibrary.org/JFK/JFK-in-History/Civil-Rights-Movement.aspx.

PHILLIP BELL, JR., MA: MA/African-American Studies/Counseling, BA/Psychology, Author, Entrepreneur, Inventor, Lecturer, Actor, Educator, Athlete, Spiritual and Fitness Activist. "©Phillip Bell, Jr. MA

BLACK PIONEERS: Hamilton, Steven. "NURTURING RECONCILIATION: Celebrating Black History Month." *Vineyard Justice Network*, 23 Feb. 2017, vineyardjusticenetwork.org/nurturing-reconciliation-celebrating-black-history-month/.

CIVIL RIGHTS CHAMPIONS: Zirin, Dave. "Dr. Martin Luther King, Muhammad Ali and What Their Secret Friendship Teaches Us Today." *The Nation*, 15 Jan. 2016, www.thenation.com/article/dr-martin-luther-king-muhammad-ali-and-what-their-secret-friendship-teaches-us-today/.

Rosa Parks

Jesse Jackson